God's Grace

other books by luis palau

GOD IS RELEVANT

WHERE IS GOD WHEN BAD THINGS HAPPEN?

God's Grace

Pictures and Portraits of True Miracles

Luis Palau

with Mike Yorkey

TESTAMENT BOOKS

NEW YORK

This 2007 edition is published by Testament Books, an imprint of
Random House Value Publishing, by agreement with Doubleday,
both divisions of Random House, Inc., New York.

Testament Books is a registered trademark and the colophon is a
trademark of Random House, Inc.

Random House
New York • Toronto • London • Sydney • Auckland
www.randomhouse.com

Printed and bound in the United States of America.

A catalog record for this title is available from the Library of Congress.

ISBN: 978-0-517-22933-0

10 9 8 7 6 5 4 3 2 1

· contents ·

Introduction   *1*

1. A PORTRAIT: *seizing an opportunity*   5

2. A PICTURE: *the water filter*   *11*

3. A PICTURE: *letters to a stranger*   *15*

4. A PICTURE: *beyond the norm*   20

5. A PORTRAIT: *busing their way to history*   26

6. A PICTURE: *"trust me"*   *31*

7. A PICTURE IN A PORTRAIT: *choosing a different road*   36

8. A PORTRAIT: *the three storks*   40

9. A PICTURE: *the andes mechanic*   45

10. A PORTRAIT: *open doors once more*   50

11. A PICTURE: *believe it or not*   54

12. A PORTRAIT: *moving mountains*   59

13. A PICTURE: *the guardian*   65

14. A PICTURE: *armed and ready*   71

15. A PORTRAIT: *down to the wire*   77

16. A PORTRAIT: *back home at last*   82

17. A PICTURE: *a heart to save*   88

18. A PORTRAIT: *nothing was wasted*   92

19. A PORTRAIT: *the teddy bear*   100

20. A PICTURE: *on the heels of an angel*   104

21. A PORTRAIT: *father's day*   108

22. A PORTRAIT: *waiting in the wings*   113

23. A PICTURE IN A PORTRAIT: *wheels up*   118

24. A PORTRAIT: *peggie's place*   123

25. A PICTURE: *turning a corner*   127

26. A PORTRAIT: *listening to God*   131

27. A PICTURE: *cartoon character*   136

28. A PICTURE: *the wake-up call*   141

29. A PICTURE IN A PORTRAIT: *living in God's economy*   146

30. A PICTURE: *october sky*   150

31. A PICTURE IN A PORTRAIT: *the hiding place*   155

32. A PORTRAIT IN THE MAKING: *total turnaround*   161

33. A PICTURE: *the house on the hill*   166

34. A PORTRAIT: *not in vain*   170

35. A PICTURE: *dutch treat*   175

36. A PICTURE: *in the rough*   180

37. A PICTURE IN A PORTRAIT: *one untimely born*   184

38. A PICTURE: *pennies from heaven*   189

39. A PICTURE: *the last-minute enrollment*   192

40. A PICTURE IN A PORTRAIT: *the unexpected trade* 197

41. A PICTURE: *hitchhiking to a safe place* 202

42. A PORTRAIT: *a better sense* 207

43. A PORTRAIT: *a child shall lead them* 210

44. A PORTRAIT: *to latvia with love* 214

45. A PICTURE AND A PORTRAIT: *over the years* 219

Acknowledgments 225

We'd Love to Hear from You! 227

More True Stories! 229

God's Grace

· *introduction* ·

God moves in a mysterious way
His wonders to perform.
   —*William Cowper, English poet (1731–1800)*

I love meeting people because, sooner or later, they want to tell me a story.

"Luis, you won't believe what happened to me," they begin, and what unfolds is a story of a gripping, personal, and often miraculous series of circumstances that only the Creator of the Universe could orchestrate.

What you're about to read are stories of how God has worked in the lives of dozens of individuals. Each of these true accounts illustrates something about God's grace, His greatness, His goodness, and His faithfulness.

You will find three types of stories in this book.

First, you will find *pictures*. Snapshots might be a better word. They are short and powerful word sketches, intended to show that God is intimately concerned with the short-term details of His special and unique creation . . . you! They show how God intervened in the normal stuff of life. Since that's where you and I live most of the time, you'll be inspired to see God's concern for the details.

Second, you will find *portraits*. If you've ever seen one of the large paintings of individuals by DaVinci or Rembrandt, you know that they contain incredible amounts of detail. You can tell by looking at one that it likely took months or even years to complete, and the result was a masterpiece. Likewise, God is creating a masterpiece out of my life, as well as yours. And a masterpiece means effort in the detail.

Third, you will find *pictures in a portrait*. This means that the events of the story shared, though perhaps a small part in someone's life, contributed to its overall course.

I believe you'll find this particular collection of stories to be a lot like life—the mundane combined with the heart-wrenching instances that mark a life forever.

Before I tell you more, let me ask two questions.

First, are you patient with God, or do you like fast-food answers to the deeper issues of life?

When I'm at the end of my rope—and I've been there many times—there's nothing I want more from God than an immediate answer. Sometimes He has sent it . . . and many times He hasn't. I'll tell you plainly: one purpose of this book is to help you be patient with God. I've discovered that His timetable for answering your most difficult circumstances will rarely fit yours. The rea-

son? It takes time—and trial—to build you into th
are meant to be—a masterpiece. As many people
will quickly admit, the miracle of answered pray
most when God is given time to do His work. At the
deepest trial, did they want a positive resolution th
immediate? Absolutely! But many on the other
unique yet common dilemmas of life—some who
two, five, or twenty years for the answer they longe
not trade God's timing for the cheap and easy out
was the ultimate answer. They learned too much tha
ness to their life, and too many of life's deepest qu
answered. Thus they could teach their loved ones th
of all: that God is *always* great, *always* good, and *alwa*

Second, do you really believe God cares about
book, you'll discover the answer should be an unequ

I've seen clear evidence of God at work in my ow
made the choice to trust my todays and tomorrows t
Jesus Christ, at a Christian camp in the Argentine
was twelve years old. From my earliest memories, I
He was making of me . . . a masterpiece. Not a p
pointed at and admired as hundreds of tourists do i
ums, but one that causes someone to point back to th
is the Master, the One who patiently and lovingly
portrait of what you see today.

Sadly, many people do not believe God is in the business of making a masterpiece of them. And why not? They hear stories of angels and miracles—the sudden recovery of a terminally ill child or the unexpected check arriving in the mail—and wonder why those events always happen to *other* people. If God doesn't perform an instant miracle at a person's time of need, does it mean He *isn't* working? That He doesn't love him or her? That He doesn't care?

If you are not sure whether God is near or far away, this book is for you. Whether you're in church more often than the church custodian or the road to your Sunday attendance is paved with good intentions, I pray that these true stories will boost your confidence that God doesn't take coffee breaks. He's painting tens, hundreds, if not thousands of brushstrokes to make your life's masterpiece.

I have reserved two stories at the end that to me represent brush strokes that have made my life what it is today. But for now, let me get right into the stories of real people who have experienced "God things" themselves.

A PORTRAIT

1.

· *seizing an opportunity* ·

Worry and deep concern for a loved one does not demonstrate a lack of faith in God. They are actually the very emotions that can serve to draw us to Him at critical hours of need. Have you ever been worried sick you were about to lose someone close? If so, you know, as Phil Callaway's story demonstrates, that when you're at the end of answers, love—and faith—sometimes find a way.

"Daddy, is Mama going to die?"

Five-year-old Stephen asked the question that Phil Callaway for years had dismissed far too casually. The woman he loved deeply had warned him of the trouble that could lie ahead.

When Phil and Ramona were in the "serious dating mode," they talked about marriage and kids and where they were going to live and what they wanted to do with their lives. At one point, Ramona had stood and paced the floor.

"What's wrong?" Phil asked.

"There's something you should know," Ramona replied anxiously. "I may have a rare disease called Huntington's. My dad had it, and I've been told that I have a fifty-fifty chance of getting it. Huntington's causes mental and physical deterioration and seizures, and if you get it, you usually die young. I just thought before we get too much further along . . ."

"I'd like to marry you someday, Ramona. I love you."

Phil never gave Huntington's disease much more thought. They were young. Invincible. And fertile. Three children were born in thirty-six months, which caused Phil to quip one day:

"Ramona, sure, we have three kids, but do you know why we're far more satisfied than the guy who has three million dollars?"

"No, why?"

"Well, the guy with three million wants more!"

Before long, however, life wasn't so funny. Ramona began waking up and pacing the floor in the middle of the night.

"What's wrong?" Phil asked through half-open eyes.

"I'm fine. I just can't sleep."

By that time, three of Ramona's six siblings had been diagnosed with Huntington's, and she was convinced she was next. The symptoms were there: lack of sleep, irritability, occasional clumsiness, even a craving for sweets.

A few weeks later Phil, the editor of *Servant* magazine in Alberta, Canada, took a phone call at his desk.

"Hello?"

Silence for five seconds.

"Hello?"

"H-h-h-elp me, please help me," Ramona cried. "I don't know what's happening."

Phil drove home in record time and burst through the door. He found his preschool children sitting on the kitchen floor, pouring cereal into bowls. "Is Mama going to die?" asked Stephen, the oldest.

Ramona lay on the living room sofa, an ugly gash on her left leg—the result of her sudden fall against a wooden bed frame—dripping blood on the carpet.

Staring with vacant eyes, she asked, "What day is it? Monday."

It's Friday, Phil thought.

"She's making funny noises," Stephen said. "She thinks I'm her dad."

Phil gathered the three children and held them close. "Maybe we should tell Jesus," said Rachael, who was three. "Maybe He can do something."

Squeezing them tightly, Phil prayed out loud: "Dear God,

help Mommy to be okay. And thank you that you're right here with us all the time."

After Phil wrapped his wife's leg and called his parents, he was searching for the doctor's phone number when Ramona let out an agonized moan. Phil watched in horror as her back arched and her head snapped back. Her face turned gray, and she slumped to the floor.

Ramona's arms and legs thrashed as Phil tried to calm her and keep her from biting her tongue. Ramona's mother, who had just arrived, called for paramedics. While Phil rode in the ambulance and held his wife's hand, he recalled reading an interview with singer Linda Ronstadt, in which she said, "I'll never get married. There's too much potential for pain."

I guess I finally understand what she meant.

The battery of tests began. CAT scans. EEGs. No clear diagnosis could be given, and Ramona returned home as doctors sorted out the conflicting signals. Meanwhile, over the next eighteen months, Ramona experienced dozens of seizures. Then some good news: doctors said a test had been developed to isolate the Huntington's gene.

On February 14, 1994, Phil and Ramona stood in the doctor's office while a doctor opened an envelope that held the test results.

"Ramona, you have the normal gene."

8

"We don't have Huntington's?" Phil asked.

"You don't have it."

The Callaways hugged the doctor. Ramona was clear. The disease would not be passed on to their children.

As the months dragged on, however, the seizures worsened. Ramona's weight slipped to ninety pounds, and people barely recognized her. Phil wondered if she would make it past her thirtieth birthday.

One day as they drove to visit Ramona's sister, another seizure laid Ramona out in the front seat. The children cowered in the back seat, crying.

"Is Mama going to die?" asked Rachael.

"I don't know," her father said. "But you know what? God says He'll always be with us. And He's never broken a promise. We can tell Him we're scared."

Yet late at night, it was Phil who could not sleep. A sense of panic built within him. "What do I do now, Lord? Where do we go from here?"

Bible verses memorized long ago offered comfort. "God is our refuge and strength, an ever-present help in trouble. Therefore we will not fear . . ." (Psalm 46:1–2).

By the fall of 1996, the seizures were occurring daily, sometimes hourly. Phil rarely left Ramona's side. Once, when she was finally asleep, he paced their dark backyard, then fell to his knees. "God!" he cried out. "I can't take it anymore. Please do something!"

As he stood, a doctor's name came to mind. Although this man attended the same church as the Callaways, Phil had never thought to ask him his opinion. Within minutes, Phil had him on the phone and was describing Ramona's symptoms.

"It sounds like something I've seen before," the doctor said. "Bring her first thing in the morning."

Phil hadn't really believed in miracles before. But within a week, Ramona was a different person. The doctor diagnosed a rare chemical deficiency and prescribed an antiseizure medication. The seizures ended. Ramona's eyes lit up with the sparkle that had first attracted him to her. Their children don't have to worry anymore that their mom will black out; that she could die at any moment. Instead, there is normalcy. So much normalcy, it brings tears to Phil's eyes to realize where they'd been . . . and where they are. Miracles do happen.

"God gave me back my wife."

Praise the Lord, [who] heals all my diseases.
He ransoms me from death and surrounds me
with love and tender mercies (Psalm 103:2–4).

A PICTURE

2.

· *the water filter* ·

If you look for them, you'll find that "love letters" come in all shapes and sizes. A picture drawn by a preschooler, a surprise check in the mail, and a clean house after a long day at work all say the same thing: I love you. The time after a loved one leaves—for whatever reason—is often the time when we need a love note the most; something tangible to hold on to. Be ready for that note, because such "God things" are everywhere!

This is not shaping up to be a cheery holiday season, Susan Wilkinson thought as she flipped through a thick stack of mail. Three months earlier, her husband, Marty, had lost a valiant fight against cancerous melanoma. He drew his final breath on August 2, 1995, at the age of forty-nine; an obituary in the *Houston Chronicle* noted that he was survived by his wife, Susan, and three children under the age of eleven.

Susan continued to sort through the mail. Nothing stopped the reminder of the crowning blow of the last three months: just five weeks after Marty's death, her mother had succumbed to lung cancer.

Lord, how am I going to get through this holiday season without Marty and Mom? Susan felt sick to her stomach as she contemplated seeing the empty seats on Thanksgiving Day and Christmas morning.

Susan opened a few bills, then held up a notice from Sterling Springs, a water filtration company. Like many Texas families, the Wilkinsons used a canister that filtered impurities from their kitchen tap water—and improved its taste. "It's time to change your filter!" said the notice, listing a phone number customers could call to order one.

The thought of ordering a simple filter was almost too much for Susan to bear. Marty had been the do-it-yourself guy around the house, the man's man who mowed the lawn, changed the sprinkler heads, fixed leaky plumbing, and had even made their son's wooden cradle in his workshop in the garage.

The thought of her "honey-do" list falling on her own shoulders greatly discouraged Susan. With a sigh, she ordered the new water filter. Three weeks after it arrived, she still had no idea what to do with it. One Saturday morning, however,

Susan decided to tackle the project. Their water was tasting pretty bad.

She turned the canister over and saw a label. Something was written in her husband's script: "November 4, 1994." *Hmm. Marty had changed that filter.* But right after the date was another inscription: "I love you."

When Susan saw the message, she stepped back and blinked hard, then drew a large breath. Such a simple message felt like a kiss from heaven, a tangible reminder of Marty's love for her months after he was gone.

Susan thought it through. Marty had learned on October 28, 1994, that his melanoma was malignant and incurable. "Two percent live five years," one of his doctors said. "But you're young, and we'll give it everything we've got."

It wouldn't be enough. Both Marty and Susan knew that his chances for surviving another year were slim, because the October biopsy revealed that the cancer was "very aggressive."

Two weeks after learning his condition was terminal, Marty changed the water filter. Knowing that the odds were poor that he would be around to change the filter again, he penned a short missive of love to his wife, knowing that she would find it.

Susan peeled off the label and tucked it into her prayer journal. After drying her eyes, she thanked God for giving Marty the idea to make a profound yet bittersweet expression of love after his death.

> . . . the sorrows of widowhood will be remembered no
> more, for your Creator is your husband. The Lord
> Almighty is his name! (Isaiah 54:4–5).

A PICTURE

3.

· *letters to a stranger* ·

Many think God wants to do only "big things" through them, that the "little things" don't matter all that much. In God's economy, the littlest things often become big things. Availability is like yeast in the hand of God. He makes your smallest bit of concern grow to make an impact in this life . . . and often for eternity. Do you want to see "God things" around you? Then tell Him you're available.

"Lord, I have so little to give back to you," Susan Morin prayed one Sunday at church. "It seems like I'm always asking you to meet my needs or answer my prayers. But Lord, what can I do for you?"

Susan, a single mom of three teenagers, was finding it hard to cope with her children's emotional needs and her precarious financial situation. Nevertheless, she longed to serve God in a way that made a difference for eternity, even though she had so little spare time to give.

The answer seemed so simple. She could pray. Susan committed to pray during her forty-five-minute commute from New Hampshire to her workplace in Vermont.

"Lord, will you give me some people to pray for?" she asked the next day as she drove to work. "I don't even have to know their needs. Just let me know who they are."

Susan arrived at the Mary Meyer Corporation, a company that makes stuffed animals. She was in charge of accounts receivable, a job that included opening the mail and preparing the bank deposits. She opened an envelope and found a note attached to a check. "I'm sorry this payment is late. I have been seriously ill. Thank you, Beverly Thompson."*

You want me to pray for her, don't you, Lord?

So began Susan's journey of praying for Beverly Thompson. At first she found it awkward to pray for someone she didn't know. She knew that Beverly owned a bookstore in Presque Isle, Maine, from where she ordered the company's plush animals to sell. But how old was she? Was she married? Did she have any children? Was her illness terminal?

Sometimes, as Susan prayed for Beverly, she found herself in tears. She prayed that Jesus would give Beverly comfort for what-

---

*Beverly Thompson is a pseudonym.

ever she had to endure. She pleaded for Beverly to find strength and courage to accept things that she might find hard to face.

A month or two passed, and Susan considered sending Beverly a card. This was risky—she could lose her job if Beverly was offended and complained to the company.

"Lord, I've grown to love Beverly Thompson," Susan prayed one morning. "I know you'll take care of me no matter what happens."

In her first card, Susan told Beverly a little about herself and how she had asked the Lord for specific people to pray for. Then she mentioned how she came across her name. She also said that God knew what Beverly was going through and loved her deeply.

Beverly never answered that letter, nor did she respond to the subsequent notes and cards Susan mailed that summer. But Susan never stopped praying for Beverly and even told her Tuesday night Bible study group about her.

Susan really was hoping Beverly would respond. She was curious what Beverly thought about this stranger and her stream of notes. Did Beverly think she was completely crazy? Did she hope that Susan would stop?

Six months passed. On a bitterly cold January evening, the phone rang. "Mom, it's for you!" fifteen-year-old Tajin hollered.

"Who is it?" Susan asked. She was tired after a long day. Actually, it had been a long month. Her car had died five days before Christmas, and she had lost a week's pay because of illness.

"It's someone named Bob Thompson," Tajin said.

Bob Thompson . . . ?

At first the name didn't register, but then Susan remembered, *Yes, Beverly Thompson. It must be her husband.*

She took the phone from her son; her hands became clammy. *I know why he's calling. He's calling to tell me to stop bothering his wife. They probably think I'm a religious kook.*

"Hello, Mr. Thompson," she squeaked.

"Hello, Susan," he replied. "My daughter and I have just been going through my wife's things, and we found your cards and notes, along with your phone number. We wanted to call and let you know how much they meant to Beverly before she died."

"Oh, I'm so sorry."

"We found your cards and notes tied up with a red ribbon," he said. "I know she must have read them, because they looked very worn."

"That's very nice, Mr. Thompson. Can you tell me more about your wife?"

"At the age of forty-eight, Beverly was diagnosed with lung cancer, which spread to her brain. She never suffered any pain at all. I know that this was the result of your prayers."

Then Mr. Thompson answered the question in Susan's heart.

18

"You may be wondering about this," he said, "but our relationship with God amounted to going to church once in a while. Church was nothing that had much effect on our lives. But that changed after Beverly began receiving your notes. I want you to know that she asked to be baptized two weeks before she passed away. The night before Beverly died she told me it was okay for her to die, because she was going home to be with her Lord."

Because Susan made herself available to God, she had made an eternal difference to a woman she never knew.

> The earnest prayer of a righteous person has great
> power and wonderful results (James 5:16b).

A PICTURE

4.

· *beyond the norm* ·

Many Christians believe the Bible when it says to go "to the ends of the earth" to share their faith. Oftentimes, when faith in God meets obedience to His Word, the path ahead is dimly lit. Reliance upon God to direct your steps is the best—and only—course. Has God ever told you to go, however, without giving you directions? He did so with the two women in this story.

Before the December 1989 revolution and execution of dictator Nicolae Ceausescu, Romanian Christians risked their lives by making any expression of faith. That didn't stop Norm Miller, CEO of Interstate Battery System of America, and his wife, Anne. The couple made several trips behind the Iron Curtain.

On one trip without her husband, Anne teamed up with a friend, Sherry, in Vienna. They entered Romania as tourists but intended to lead women's Bible studies. In their purses was the address of a pastor and his family. After knocking on the door, they were greeted warmly and shown inside.

"Did anyone see you?" the pastor inquired.

"No, we don't think so," Anne replied.

"Good. It will be less risky if you stay inside."

For two days, the cloistered American women observed how their counterparts lived in Romania. All women worked outside the home. They began the day at five-thirty A.M. by standing in bread lines, arrived at work at seven, left at four, went home to household chores, and then fell into bed exhausted.

Every meal except one followed the same menu: a plate lined with fatty summer sausages and goat cheese, filled in the middle with tomatoes and cucumbers. Anne and Sherry ate sparingly, wondering if they were taking food from the mouths of their hosts, who had two small children. They did not butter their bread, because they knew the monthly ration was just one kilo.

Each night, the pastor's home filled with women who came to hear Anne and Sherry teach biblical concepts regarding child rearing and building a marriage. The women eagerly took notes and asked questions. Meetings closed with fervent prayers and quiet singing.

Romanian law prohibited religious meetings. Conversing with Westerners was also illegal, as was religious literature. So the meetings were secret, and the women diligently hand-copied all the materials.

The time came for Anne and Sherry to travel by train to the next city. They were told to wear dark clothing, eschew makeup and jewelry, avoid eye contact, and try to blend in as best they could.

Because their train trip involved several tricky changes, Anne and Sherry worried whether they would find the right city and the people expecting them. They boarded their train at five-thirty A.M. and looked for an empty compartment where they could munch on granola bars and drink orange juice—a "luxurious" Western breakfast. They found a compartment, took their seats, and started to open their overnight bags containing their food. Before they could begin eating, however, four more people piled into the compartment. That meant no talking (a dead giveaway that they were Americans), no reading, and no eating their foreign food.

Two hours into the journey the train stopped at a station. The conductor bellowed out the name of the town as he walked through the train. Sherry, who was responsible for the travel arrangements, glanced at Anne and shook her head, but in the back of her mind, she wondered if they had missed the right town. She silently prayed, asking not to make the wrong turns . . . or the wrong moves.

A few minutes later, the conductor yelled out the name of the next stop. A young woman sitting across from Anne had been sleeping, but she suddenly awakened and stopped the conductor. She seemed to be asking questions about the next stop.

When the train rolled into the station, the young woman stood up, grabbed her belongings, and nodded at Anne as if to say, "Follow me." Sherry and Anne shot each other panicked looks, yet they somehow knew they should follow.

They stood behind the woman as she took her place among waiting passengers on the station platform. Ten minutes passed. Another train pulled in. The young woman glanced at the Americans and said one word in English: "Accident."

Anne and Sherry wondered why this young woman had picked them out as Americans when they had not uttered a word in English or done anything to draw attention to themselves. When she boarded the train, the two Americans dutifully followed.

No backing out now! Anne thought.

The train was a "local," stopping in every town and city along its route. After three hours of traveling, the young woman looked over at Sherry, caught her eye, and nodded. The train braked to a stop, and they saw the name of the town they were supposed to go to on the sign above the platform. Anne and Sherry stood and left, while the train transporting "their angel" disappeared down the track, leaving the Americans alone again in a strange city.

"What do you think is going to happen next?" Anne asked.

"With God there is always another surprise around the corner," Sherry replied. "Plan A was for someone to meet us, but I don't see anyone."

"Well, what's Plan B?"

"Don't you remember?" asked Sherry. "We were supposed to stand in the waiting area with a newspaper under one arm."

"Is there a Plan C?"

"If all else fails, we're to walk out of the station and turn right."

Anne prayed for guidance. She had been praying for three years to take this trip to teach Romanian Christians. Couldn't God be trusted to shine a light on the path they were supposed to take to the next pastor's house?

They left the train station and started walking down the street.

"Where are we going?" asked Sherry.

"God is going to lead us where we need to go," said Anne.

After a block, Anne said, "Let's turn right here." Two blocks later, she sensed she was to turn right again.

"There it is!" she exclaimed. God had led them straight to the pastor's front door.

Trust in the Lord with all your heart; do not depend on
your own understanding. Seek his will in all you do, and
he will direct your paths (Proverbs 3:5–6).

A PORTRAIT

5.

· *busing their way to history* ·

One of the most important prayers is asking for God's direction. While there are always mid-course corrections throughout life, you never know how God will answer that prayer. Have you ever asked God to direct your steps? A man named Cliff did. Fifty years later he's on the same path, and he's never looked back.

Married all of three days to Cliff, Billie Barrows was worried about where they were going to spend the night. Brides have a way of wanting to know those things.

"We could go to Wisconsin Dells," Cliff offered.

"Wisconsin? What about that resort hotel at Lake Lure?"

"Yes, we could go there, and it's not too far from here," Cliff said.

They agreed their next bus destination would be North Carolina's Blue Ridge Mountains. Just before the young couple left their motel room on that June day in 1945, they asked the Lord to give them a safe trip to Lake Lure, a few hours away.

Cliff and Billie, who was still a student at Bob Jones College in Greenville, South Carolina, a year after Cliff had graduated, were on their honeymoon.

With two suitcases, the couple set out on their next adventure. The bus dropped them off in a nearby town, and some kind strangers picked them up and dropped them off at Lake Lure, where they discovered the military had taken over the hotel. World War II, finally winding down in Europe, was still raging in the Pacific.

A Christian couple invited Cliff and Billie to stay with them. For the next few days, they swam in Lake Lure and climbed to the top of Chimney Rock.

"Well, we need to be moving along," Cliff told his hosts.

"Where are you going?"

"I don't know. Where are we going, Billie?"

Before she could respond, one of their hosts said, "We know a family in Asheville, less than an hour from here. The Browns would enjoy having you stay with them. Let me call and ask. The Browns have a daughter you might know—Hortense. She's a student at Bob Jones College."

"We know Hortense," Cliff said. "It will be nice to meet her family."

So it was off to Asheville. At the city's municipal pool, Cliff and Billie bumped into a man named Jim Adair, whom Cliff also had met at Bob Jones.

"What are you doing here?" Cliff asked.

"Working. I'm a reporter at the *Asheville Times*," said Jim. Although they hadn't known each other well at college, Jim had admired Cliff's energetic song leading.

The next day, Jim's pastor, Reverend Julian Bandy, called. "A young evangelist is in town," he said. "He wants to play some golf this afternoon. Care to join us?"

"Sure," said the cub reporter.

On the first tee, the tall, lanky evangelist, wearing a red golf cap, introduced himself. "Hi," he said. "I'm Billy Graham."

"Jim Adair."

The loop around the golf course went quickly, as Billy played "ready golf" and rarely took much time to make his shots. Reverend Bandy had honors for most of the eighteen holes.

At dinnertime, Jim received a phone call from his new golfing buddy. "Do you know someone who could lead singing for me tonight?" asked the earnest evangelist, who was scheduled to preach that night. "My song leader was unexpectedly called back to Chicago."

Jim suggested a friend of his, and Billy said, "Sounds fine to me."

As soon as he hung up, Jim thought about Cliff Barrows and his enthusiastic singing in college, and he remembered that Billy said he was speaking at a youth event. Maybe a younger man would be better, and besides, he played a mean trombone . . .

Jim called Billy back. "I think I know someone, a younger fellow, who would be a better fit. His name is Cliff Barrows, and he happens to be in town on his honeymoon."

"Well, if he can lead the singing, then send him out."

"I'll get on it."

Jim phoned the Brown residence and asked for Cliff. Then he looked at his watch. The event was only hours away.

After relaying Billy Graham's request, Jim asked Cliff if he was available.

"Sounds good," said Cliff, "but let me check with Billie."

After a minute, Cliff returned to the phone. "She says it's fine, and she plays a good piano. We'll ride out to the auditorium with the Browns."

That evening, the auditorium pulsated with enthusiastic singing as Cliff directed and Billie played the piano. Afterward, Billy Frank, as some people called the young evangelist from Charlotte, preached with vigor.

That was the start of a long friendship between Cliff Barrows and Billy Graham. A year later, Billy asked the couple to join his crusade team. For more than a half century, Cliff was the world-renowned evangelist's song leader and right-hand man, helping bring the good news of Jesus Christ to millions.

We can make our plans, but the Lord
determines our steps (Proverbs 16:9).

A PICTURE

6.

· *"trust me"* ·

Whether you're faithful or faithless, there are times when it is truly difficult to believe God can provide. While many of us have never had to worry about where the next day's food would come from, or next month's rent, there have been days in our history when such worry was the norm. Along with this constant unknown came a deep dependence upon the Unseen Guest. If you knew the resources—and the character—of this Guest, any doubts about God's power would disappear . . . as they did for Susan and Andrew . . .

Susan Warren's breath crystallized and sparkled in the rays of dawn creeping into the bedroom. The freezing temperature that January morning encouraged her to tug the comforter up to her nose. Then she snuggled closer to her sleeping husband, Andrew. That movement awakened her unborn baby, who stretched and kicked inside her abdomen.

A few moments later, sunlight trumpeted through the flimsy curtains. Susan tapped Andrew lightly.

"It's time to get up," she said. "Please go light the heater."

Their one-bedroom cinder-block home was a mere five hundred square feet, and the old kerosene heater struggled like a mighty warrior against the drafts that assaulted the cracks in the fifty-year-old house. During the day, with sunlight as an ally, the heater kept their house toasty warm and comfortable. At night they let the old soldier flicker out, preferring instead the brisk Tennessee air.

Andrew groaned and rolled out of bed. Susan heard him shuffle to the family room, then strike a match. The crackle of the wick warmed Andrew's hands as it heated to a cherry-red glow.

As quickly as the wick came to life, it died. That could mean only one thing.

"We're low on fuel!" Andrew hollered. "I'm going to fill up the tank."

Susan heard the back door slam. A fifty-gallon barrel in the backyard held their winter supply of kerosene. Andrew knew it was more than half full—plenty to get them through the winter.

Susan slipped out of bed and tiptoed to check on their son, sleeping in his crib. His blond hair curled against his face, and a slight sweat glistened on his brow from the heat of the double layer of pajamas he wore. Susan leaned on the door frame, her hand on the life growing within her, and thanked God for providing for their needs during their lean college years.

Andrew was a full-time student in his final year of aviation school; Susan had opted to stay home with their son. Andrew's sideline, auto-repair jobs helped keep food on their table and pay their rent, but they rarely had anything left in the bank at month's end. Their last forty dollars had just paid the electric bill.

The back door slammed again. When Susan turned and looked at Andrew, her mouth went dry. He had carried in a load of worry and despair. "Our barrel has a leak. The kerosene is gone."

They stood there in silence, listening to fear keep the beat with their hearts. They had no money in the cookie jar; they were eating corn bread left over from the Wednesday night church supper. What were they going to do?

"We'd better pray," Andrew said quietly. As he asked the Lord to rescue them, Susan's heart stormed. Dismay buffeted her faith. Through the rain she heard a voice thunder in her soul, "Trust me," but she could not see past the dark clouds to hold on to her Savior.

Andrew left for school while Susan started on the housework. A chill invaded the house. Susan bundled her son in another layer and tried to pray again, but all she could feel were waves of despair, tossing her about in an ocean of doubt.

Shortly after lunch, a friend stopped by and asked if Andrew could repair his pickup. He handed Susan the keys and said something about leaving town for the weekend. "I'll come for the truck Monday."

Well, that will help us buy some groceries, Susan thought.

When Andrew arrived home two hours later, the house was cold, but a warm smile flickered on his face.

"Guess what we got in our mailbox at school?" he said. He handed Susan an envelope. Inside were two crisp twenty-dollar bills. "Money for the kerosene."

"From whom?"

Andrew shrugged and shook his head. "I don't know." Then his smile faded. "But how are we going to fit the barrel into our hatchback?"

It was Susan's turn to smile. She dangled the pickup keys in front of his wide eyes.

While Andrew loaded the barrel into the truck, Susan searched the envelope for evidence of the identity of their bene-factor. A slip of paper was folded between the twenties. She pulled it out, and a chill rippled through her. The note said, "Proverbs 3:5—Trust in the Lord with all your heart."

And this same God who takes care of me
will supply all your needs from his
glorious riches (Philippians 4:19a).

7.

· *choosing a different road* ·

You've heard the phrase "you've made your bed, now lie in it."
Perhaps you've also heard "what you sow, you'll reap." Both
speak of facing consequences for reckless behavior. Yes, there
are physical consequences of poor decisions, and sometimes
those consequences are tough to swallow. But the emotional re-
sults—no matter how debilitating or long-lasting—can serve to
point you toward choosing one of two alternatives: prison or
freedom. A mill worker in Washington State faced choosing one
of those alternatives after a terrible accident.

They called it the "green chain" at the Aloha Cedar Products
sawmill outside Hoquiam, Washington. For five days a week,
eight hours a day, Bob Mortimer pulled freshly sawn 2 by 4 boards
and 6 by 6 beams off the roller belt and stacked them for shipping.

At twenty-one years old, Bob didn't mind the physically de-
manding work. It fit well with the blue-collar lifestyle of drinking

Rainier longnecks and getting stoned with his buddies after quitting time.

Bob was sixteen when he tried to wake up his father in their single-wide trailer home—and couldn't. He had died from a drug overdose, and when the family moved to the Pacific Northwest to start over, Bob found himself drinking and doping with a new group of friends.

Some of those friends worked at the sawmill and, after partying one night in Olympia, Bob and his brother, Tom, started the drive back home to Hoquiam, fifty miles away. Tom took a curve wrong, overcorrected, and struck a power pole before sliding down an embankment.

The brothers were lucky this time; they emerged from the car unscathed.

"You okay?" Tom asked.

"Believe so," said Bob, stepping out of the car. "Where's the road?"

"Dunno."

"Did we hit a tree?"

"I don't know what we hit," Tom said.

Bob saw a path to the highway through the knocked-down brush.

When he climbed the embankment and reached the road, Bob didn't realize that waiting for him were five downed power lines. In the darkness his left arm touched a line, causing 12,500 volts of electricity to surge through his body. He fell to his knees, which grounded him. The electrical charge, looking for somewhere to go, exploded out of his knees. He fell forward across the other wires, which burned the front of his body.

When Tom came upon his brother, Bob wasn't moving. Tom figured Bob was dead, so he sat on the side of the road and wondered what to do next. Then Bob moaned. Tom pulled him free and kept him alive until help arrived.

The next morning Bob woke up at Harbor View Medical Center in Seattle and signed a release to amputate his left arm. Two weeks later doctors took his right leg. He kept his left leg several months before surrendering it.

Bob endured six months of recuperation and rehabilitation at the Seattle hospital while doctors grafted skin over his burns. Following his release, Bob returned to the only world he knew— drinking and drugs. This time around, he drank beer and smoked marijuana to blunt the pain of being a triple amputee.

He was twenty-five when he met Darla Hollis, who was babysitting his sister's children. They were chatting one day when Darla said, "Would you like to go to church with me sometime?"

Hey, my life's so messed up. Why not? Bob thought.

That Sunday in church, Bob heard the good news of Jesus Christ for the first time. When the pastor invited listeners to allow God to take control of their lives, Bob thought back to the decisions that had framed his life. When he chose his own way, he lost his limbs and burned his body. When he allowed others to choose his path, he lost his dignity and pride. *What more can I lose? Why don't I let God lead the way?*

Bob didn't think twice. He rolled his wheelchair to the front of the church. That morning Bob repented of his party lifestyle and hard heart, and he surrendered his life to Jesus Christ.

Six months later Bob rolled his wheelchair down the church aisle once more, this time waiting for Darla, dressed in a white wedding gown.

Nearly twenty years later, Bob can't speak about Darla without smiling. They live in Gig Harbor, Washington, with their twelve-year-old daughter, Nicole, eight-year-old son, Grant, and toddler, Chanel.

Bob travels around the country, speaking several hundred times a year to school assemblies, community organizations, and churches, ministering with a message of hope borne out of horrible tragedy.

To all who mourn . . . he will give beauty for ashes,
joy instead of mourning, praise instead of despair.
For the Lord has planted them like strong and graceful
oaks for his own glory (Isaiah 61:3).

A PORTRAIT

8.

· *the three storks* ·

God speaks the way He wants to speak. A burning bush, a donkey, an angel . . . Cover to cover, God shares His wisdom and will throughout the Bible. Some people believe God also speaks through the audible voice of another believer. If you have ever wished God could show you what to do next, then this story will open your eyes to one fact: God can be very creative when He wants to be!

Friends had warned Mary and Rolf Benirschke that a Russian adoption would be fraught with peril and meters of red tape. Sure enough, ten months passed before the Russian government notified the couple they could return to Moscow to finalize Valery's adoption.

Mary's heart had melted when she first met the shy four-year-old at a Russian orphanage. As her brother-in-law held a camcorder, Mary lifted Valery into her arms and kissed him. She bonded with him immediately.

Rolf made the trip from California this time. An interpreter and guide met him and other anxious parents-to-be at Moscow's Sheremetyevo Airport on an Easter morning in 1996 and drove to an imposing government building. Finally, Rolf's name was called.

"Did you have a pleasant flight?" asked the ministry official as he ruffled through the Benirschke file.

"Yes, I did," Rolf replied.

"Hmm, yes. Before we can proceed, Mr. Benirschke, there is one small problem."

"And what would that be?"

"It seems that Valery has a brother named Viktor. We found him in another orphanage about three hours from here. You may not be aware of this, but it's our policy not to break up families. If you want to complete the adoption of Valery, you will also have to take Viktor."

Even with jet lag, Rolf quickly figured out he was at a disadvantage. This Russian had an American on the hook—here was a way to dispatch two kids from overcrowded orphanages instead of only one.

Two children? This was not part of the plan. Rolf and Mary

already were parents of a special-needs three-year-old, Kari, who had a mild form of cerebral palsy.

"Can I meet him first?"

"By all means."

The next day, Rolf was driven to Sovietsk in a ramshackle Lada that couldn't top 40 mph. At the orphanage he was led to a community room, where two dozen pale and malnourished boys, ranging in age from two to four, were playing.

"That's him," said the orphanage director, pointing toward a corner. Rolf saw a pallid, listless boy staring into space.

"How old is he?"

"Two years, three months. He weighs eight kilos."

Seventeen, eighteen pounds, Rolf calculated, way under the chart. He also had a cleft lip that had been poorly repaired.

Most of the boys seemed happy, eager to receive gifts their visitor had brought. Viktor? He stood by himself, unresponsive. Rolf walked over and blew up a balloon. Nothing. He tickled him, tried to get him to laugh. He waved a hand in front of his face. The eyes didn't follow.

"What are you going to do?" asked Sergei, his interpreter.

"How long do I have to decide?"

"Until tomorrow."

Back at his hotel, Rolf fell to his knees and asked God for guidance. He opened the Bible and read several psalms about relying on the Lord. As much as he wanted to, he couldn't call Mary—the national phone system wasn't working.

"Father, please give me a sign one way or the other," Rolf prayed. "Show me what I should do."

When Rolf woke up the next morning, he still wasn't sure what course he would take. He continued to pray for a sign as the Lada rumbled through the countryside. Riding with Rolf were an American couple who also were receiving a child that day.

"Look, storks," said Sergei, pointing to the regal birds alongside the road.

Rolf had grown up in a bird-watching family in New Hampshire. Sergei was right, those were beautiful storks.

"We have a saying in Russia that storks bring babies," Sergei continued. "Perhaps a good omen for today, *da?*"

Rolf counted three storks walking through the marshy land. Three? *That's it,* he thought. *Three storks means three babies—one for the American couple and two for me.*

At the orphanage, he gathered up little Viktor and hugged him, tears freely flowing. "Yes, I'll take him," Rolf said. They gathered up his belongings and returned to Moscow for Valery.

Two days later, they boarded a flight for London and then New York. Once on American soil, Rolf called Mary in California.

"Honey, you know how you said you always wanted a larger family? Well, I have a little surprise for you . . ."

Renamed Erik and Timmy, the boys are thriving. Timmy (Viktor) has gained weight and has begun school.

Children are a gift from the Lord; they are
a reward from him (Psalm 127:3).

A PICTURE

9.

· *the andes mechanic* ·

Many people think prayer is complicated. They have to be in a certain place, pray in a certain position, and say just the right words for the Almighty to listen and act. The story below illustrates how the simplest prayer can bring you the miracle you need, when you need it.

The weekend getaway in Huancayo had been the perfect tonic for Esteban and Carmela Tosoni and their children, Vanessa and Marco.

Situated at a breathtaking elevation of eleven thousand feet, Huancayo is one hundred miles east of Lima, Peru's capital city. Picturesque colonial architecture draws hundreds of thousands of tourists annually to its cobblestone streets. The Tosonis had enjoyed ambling through the city's outdoor market looking at Indian textiles.

Most families began driving back to Lima by four P.M. Sunday afternoon, but the Tosonis lingered an extra hour before loading their white Nissan station wagon. Then they set off to cross the lofty Andes.

"Look, the train!" ten-year-old Vanessa exclaimed.

"That's the Centrale, built by the French and considered one of the most remarkable railroad constructions in the world," Carmela said proudly. "The Centrale is the highest railroad in the world. I remember from my school days that the train goes up to 15,800 feet. Esteban, how high will we be going today?"

"I think the top of the pass is just below that," he said. "This time of year, there's sure to be some ice."

The car suddenly lurched, and the engine coughed twice before quitting. Esteban pulled onto the shoulder of the narrow two-lane highway.

Esteban rolled up his sleeves and opened the hood. He wasn't a mechanic, but he could do a few perfunctory things—check the spark plugs or see if any hoses were broken. "I don't know what's wrong with her," he said. "She's not overheating."

The sun was starting to drop behind the mountains, and few cars were passing by. Every now and then a truck rumbled past them.

"What are we going to do?" Carmela asked.

"We are a family that believes in prayer, so I think the answer is obvious," said Esteban.

"Yes, Daddy, let's pray," Vanessa said.

"Me, too," said Marco.

The family members took turns praying aloud that God would send someone to help them.

"Look," said Marco, moments after they all opened their eyes. "Someone is coming."

"I don't see anyone," Esteban said, looking in each direction. He looked again and spotted a lonely figure walking toward them in the middle of the highway.

"See, I told you someone was out there," Marco said.

"What's he carrying?" Carmela asked.

"It looks like a box of some sort," Esteban offered.

"Maybe he works around here," said Vanessa.

"I doubt it, Vane. I don't see any houses or stores nearby," said her father.

The man walked up to their car. He looked to be in his early thirties with straight black hair but no mustache. He wore faded work pants and a shirt, along with dusty leather shoes. His right hand held a small, wooden box.

"Are you a mechanic?" Esteban asked.

"Yes, I am."

"Could you help me?"

"You want me to help you? I can do that."

The man looked under the hood of the car for a few minutes.

"You are not getting gas from the gas filter into the engine, but I can fix it for you," he said as he pulled several tools from his box and began the necessary repairs.

"See if it starts," he said to Esteban.

The engine roared to life.

"Let me help you get over that pass, because your car might quit again," said the man. "Can I drive?"

"Sure," said Esteban, who wasn't wary at all. The man seemed so kind-hearted.

The full station wagon labored but crossed the Andes over the next twenty miles. Once the car started downhill, with Lima visible in the distance, the man pulled the Nissan into a gas station.

"I will stay here," he said.

"But can't we take you home or someplace you have to go?" asked Esteban. "We don't want to leave you out here in the middle of nowhere."

"No, I will be fine."

"But let us pay you something. Surely, you are hungry and need something to eat."

"No, I will stay here," he said.

The Tosoni family waved good-bye, then started driving on toward Lima.

"Do you think he was an angel?" Carmela asked.

"I don't know for sure," Esteban said, "but now I do know God really does take care of His children."

My help comes from the Lord, who made the heavens
and the earth. He will not let you stumble or fall; the
one who watches over you will not sleep. The Lord
keeps watch over you as you come and go
(Psalm 121:2–3, 8).

A PORTRAIT

10.

· *open doors once more* ·

God is never limited by time or space in answering a prayer or accomplishing His will. That's what being omniscient means. Have you wondered if your life and faith will make a difference in succeeding generations . . . if your silent pleas for family and friends will be heeded by the hand of God? The following story is so remarkable it can only be described as a "God thing."

When Mikhail Gorbachev liberalized Russia's strict thought-control policies, no one could have guessed that two lives would intersect in a most unusual way. Dimitri, a Russian citizen, knew nothing of God and existed from day to day trying to stay alive. Silently, he blamed the Russian system for failing to bring about abundance of food and family cohesion. As a boy, he learned that many in his extended family had not escaped the brutal side of Communism.

Paul Eshleman, director of the *Jesus* Film Project for Campus

Crusade for Christ, was invited to screen the film at a Moscow film festival. Paul ended up signing a contract to show the film throughout the former Soviet republics—but for theater release only. To protect the financial investment made to bring the film to the silver screen, the contract stated that *Jesus* would not be shown on television while the film circulated in theaters.

Paul soon learned, however, that a Russian producer had sold the TV rights on the side—and pocketed the rubles. A distressing development for sure, but without it a high-ranking bureaucrat in the Soviet Ministry of Education might have missed a divine appointment.

Alexei Brudenov happened to catch the last ten minutes of *Jesus* at home on television one evening. Curious to learn more about this man named Jesus, he purchased a ticket a couple of days later at a theater whose marquee advertised the film. When he saw the Roman soldiers nail Jesus' hands to the cross, Alexei broke down and wept. He cried again at the close of the movie when he trusted Jesus Christ as his Savior.

Alexei ordered sweeping changes in the educational system. He allowed ministries and schoolteachers to come to Russia and instruct elementary and high school teachers on how to teach Christian principles and ethics to their students. Since 1991, millions of Russian children have heard the good news of Jesus Christ in the state-run schools.

When *Jesus* arrived in the city of Stavropol, Doug and Kyle Clarkson worked with a team of schoolteachers who wanted to teach a curriculum based on the Bible and show *Jesus* to their students. The team soon ran out of its supply of New Testaments. One of the teachers mentioned that a warehouse outside of town once stored Bibles confiscated from Christians in the 1930s. Multitudes of believers were sent to the gulags, where most died for being "enemies of the state."

A team member drove to the warehouse to check it out. Sure enough, the Bibles were still there. "Can we have them to distribute to the people of Stavropol?"

The next day the team returned with a truck to load Bibles. A laborer named Dimitri, an agnostic college student, had come only for the day's wages. Midway through the job the young man disappeared.

"Have you seen Dimitri?" someone asked.

"No, I haven't," replied one of the Americans. "I'll look around."

Dimitri was found weeping in a corner of the warehouse. He explained he had picked up a Bible to steal it, but what he found inside shook him to the core.

"Here," he said, pointing to the first page. "That's my grandmother's signature."

The odds of Dimitri reaching for his grandmother's Bible

were astronomical but not beyond the reach of God. Though decades separated a grandmother and her grandson, the most important message she could bring—perhaps a message she had specifically prayed for—was finally delivered in God's time and in God's way.

The results will echo in eternity.

Forever, O Lord, your word stands firm in heaven.
Your faithfulness extends to every generation, as
enduring as the earth you created. Your laws remain
true today, for everything serves your plans
(Psalm 119:89–91).

A PICTURE

11.

· *believe it or not* ·

When catastrophe strikes, as it has for millions upon millions from the beginning of recorded history, there is a natural tendency to place blame . . . usually on a higher power. But is that the correct response? Although our culture has adopted the phrase "act of God" to describe an unpredictable disaster, I believe the true "acts of God" are found in the aftermath of catastrophe in the acts of those who respond to save and comfort individuals who have been devastated. The debate will always be with us as to what—or who—causes catastrophe, but this story shows a silver lining in the inevitable clouds of trouble.

"Oh, Jesus, have mercy!" said a nameless rescuer. Then finally, "Somebody is alive!"

For the moment, Mike Redlick had survived the Loma Prieta earthquake.

It was October 17, 1989. A festive atmosphere had permeated Safeway's corporate headquarters in Oakland, California, where Mike worked as a logistics analyst. Radios had been tuned to the pre-game show of game three of the World Series between Oakland and San Francisco. The first pitch was scheduled for 5:25 P.M.

Mike looked at his watch: 4:25. Normally, he left work at 4:30 for the drive home: northbound on Interstate 880, west across the San Francisco Bay Bridge, and then south to San Bruno, where his pregnant wife, Lynn, was caring for their two preschoolers, Matt and Sean. If he left now, however, he'd get caught in the baseball traffic around Candlestick Park. *Better wait fifteen, twenty minutes,* he thought.

At 4:50, Mike walked out to his 1984 Sunbird, a root-beer-colored four-door with plenty of commuting miles on the odometer. Almost by rote, he buckled his seat belt and drove to the Cypress Freeway, Interstate 880.

The expressway was a double-decked structure elevated over the east-west grids of the streets below. Mike stepped on the gas and easily merged into lane two of the northbound lower deck. Commuter traffic usually clogged the four lanes, but on this afternoon Mike saw nothing but clear sailing. *Everyone left work early to watch the World Series,* he thought. *I've timed the drive home perfectly.*

Suddenly a vehicle bumped his car from behind. Then all

four tires flattened. In the instant his mind struggled to process what this meant, he was flung sideways and crashed through the passenger-side window.

Dazed, Mike took a few moments to focus his eyes. When he did, he realized a lot more than tire blowouts had happened. Slabs of concrete entombed his car. One huge chunk had nailed the hood, but his engine was still running. He could hear a frantic voice on the radio, announcing that a major earthquake had struck the Bay area.

Blood dripped down Mike's face from a cut on his forehead, but he didn't feel any broken bones. Pinned precariously under tons of concrete, he was unable to budge from his half-in, half-out-of-the-car position.

"God, You're in control here," he prayed. "If You want to take me, it's in Your hands. You know that I have a beautiful wife, two kids, another on the way, but if it's Your will that I not survive, I give myself to You."

Mike coughed several times from the acrid dust swirling through the air. He began screaming for help.

Minutes after the earthquake struck, residents from a nearby housing project ran to the wrecked freeway—the top deck had "pancaked" onto the lower deck, crushing cars and their occupants. Several people climbed shattered support columns, holding on to curled steel reinforcement rods that had been bent and exposed. An aftershock threatened to drop the entire freeway onto the streets below.

Mike continued to call out for help as he heard rescuers working their way toward him. Three men finally reached him.

"I can't get out," he said. "You're going to have to get the door open."

"I'll be right back," said one, who returned a few minutes later with a crowbar.

They worked the door until finally it sprang open. Mike was able to walk to safety. Sitting on a nearby sidewalk, he felt soreness in his chest. Several teeth had been chipped, but he was going to be okay. Looking north, he saw what resembled a Hollywood set for a disaster film. Flames licked the sky as emergency vehicles responded to a five-mile stretch of concrete rubble that had been the Cypress Freeway. Later, Mike would learn about the forty-one deaths and the scores of injured—some whose legs were amputated to free them.

At eight P.M., Mike phoned Lynn from the hospital where he was treated and released. A cousin from the East Bay offered to drive him home. As their car sped across the undamaged San Mateo Bridge, Mike realized he had been given a special gift—life. Why was he thrown sideways, not forward, when the car came to a sudden halt? And why wasn't the Sunbird totally crushed by tons of concrete that landed on its hood and roof?

Great questions, and ones that Mike can't answer. All he knows is that God spared his life.

> For you have rescued me from death; you have kept my
> feet from slipping. So now I can walk in your presence,
> O God, in your life-giving light (Psalm 56:13).

A PORTRAIT

12.

· *moving mountains* ·

Few have the courage to "pray big." Yet some people have an earnest desire to see God do something extraordinary in a hopeless situation. Prayers for the healing of the common cold or for a more respectful teenager—as valuable as these prayers are—simply aren't what excites them. Have you ever tried to pray a prayer that was too big for God to answer? As you'll discover—through time, persistence, and effort—there is no prayer too big for God.

What could be more foolish? Two Americans deciding to pray for twenty-five years for a continent they knew nothing about.

"We have to pray for something bigger than ourselves," Doug Coe told Bob Hunter, a new Christian who asked his friend how to pray. "Pick a city like Washington, or a state like Virginia, or a country like Russia, or even a continent like Africa. If you pray and stick with it for twenty-five years, you will see God move mountains."

For some reason, the thought of praying for Africa stuck with Bob. Several days later Bob and one of the other men in his prayer group began meeting to pray for this vast continent. First they looked at a map to learn the names of new countries that had been formed since they were in high school. Then they prayed. A couple of other men soon joined them.

Back in the 1970s Uganda was in the news. Idi Amin was executing thousands of people. So the first country the group prayed for in earnest was Uganda. Following Jesus' instruction to ask God "to send out workers into his harvest field" (Matthew 9:38), the men asked God to raise up a worker from Kampala, Uganda's capital, whom they could support.

A few days later Bob attended a retreat at a hotel near Washington. That morning it was announced a group was gathering to pray for Africa after lunch. A missionary nurse who was not attending the retreat came to pray with them. It turned out she worked at Mengo Hospital in Kampala!

Bob invited her to visit his family and go to church with them. It happened to be "Missions Sunday," and when the scheduled missionary speaker failed to show, Bob suggested that the nurse from Kampala take his place.

A few weeks later the church missions committee chairman asked Bob to find out what single monetary gift might help

Mengo Hospital most. Try as he might, Bob could not reach the Ugandan hospital via telephone, so he prayed.

The next morning Bob joined a group for breakfast. The host asked if Bob would like to meet his guest, a man from Uganda. It turned out his wife worked at Mengo Hospital, too!

Instead of giving a single gift of about $1,000, however, the missions committee decided to make Mengo Hospital an ongoing project. (In the last two decades, the church has sent about $3 million worth of supplies.)

Bob took his first trip to Uganda to visit the hospital just as Idi Amin was being pushed out as president. Convinced that helping the hospital was futile without working on reconciliation in the ravaged country, Bob met with parliamentary leaders friendly to the new president, Milton Obote, and those who opposed him. He found each side willing to meet with him but not with each other.

"Lord, how can we get these guys to sit together and heal their land?" he prayed.

The answer came quickly. During a layover at the Nairobi airport, Bob sat next to an American missionary as he waited for his plane. She was the daughter of Andrew Young, then mayor of Atlanta. She suggested that Bob call her father and ask him to visit Uganda. Bob called. Andrew Young agreed. And back to Uganda Bob went.

It worked. Bob and Andrew Young met and started a process of reconciliation. Then Bob returned to Uganda with a team that included several U.S. senators and members of the German Bundestag.

The German ambassador in Kampala asked the Bundestag members why they were wasting their time on this hopeless situation. They replied that a U.S. senator had asked them to come.

The ambassador turned to the senator and asked, "Why are you here?" The senator replied that Bob Hunter asked him to come.

"And why did you come?" Bob was asked.

"Because we are here to build a bridge of reconciliation among divided people," he said.

"Just who are the men who will be the pillars for this bridge?"

"I don't know, but God does."

Both the U.S. senators and the German ambassador rolled their eyes. "Well," Bob said, "you have all the money, all the diplomatic skill, all the power, and look at the mess in this country. Can we make it any worse?"

The reconciliation effort included opposition rebels, one of whom, Yoweri Museveni, became president in due course. A Museveni adviser who believed in Jesus Christ met with Bob, and they talked about forgiveness, reconciliation, and love for one's enemies.

President Museveni was persuaded to attend the National Prayer Breakfast in Washington, where he spoke about his relationship with Jesus Christ—"I left the official church, but never Jesus," he said. His wife's prayer brought tears to business leaders, politicians, and diplomats.

President Museveni authorized Bob to help organize a prayer breakfast for Uganda. People of every tribe, color, religion, and station attended. Speaker after speaker talked of the hate they had held for others in the country, and how much they had been changed by God.

Prior to the prayer breakfast, the president called Bob to his office and asked what he thought about the situation in South Africa. Bob replied that he thought the country was heading in the right direction after releasing Nelson Mandela from prison. President Museveni agreed.

"I am now the chairman of the Organization of African Unity," he said. "It can't be official just yet, but I want to send a delegation to South Africa to tell the leaders that love and reconciliation are the answer to the bloodshed that everyone predicts for their country. What do you think?"

"That sounds like a great idea," said Bob.

"Can you go? We need a white in the delegation to make the point we want to make."

Bob went and met with Mandela, de Klerk, Buthelezi, and

other South African leaders. He read 1 Corinthians 13, the Bible's love chapter, and Christians from Kenya, Zambia, and Uganda spoke of how forgiveness was critical to South Africa's success, and emphasized that South Africa's success was critical to the continent's prosperity. This message proved pivotal in the bloodless transition from white rule to majority rule in South Africa.

To say the least, Bob Hunter's little group is still meeting to pray for Africa. And mountains keep moving!

"I assure you, even if you had faith as small as a mustard seed you could say to this mountain, 'Move from here to there,' and it would move. Nothing would be impossible" (Matthew 17:20).

A PICTURE

13.

· *the guardian* ·

God sends His protection in hundreds of different ways. Some-times, that heavenly guard seems almost angelic. I don't pretend to understand why protection is given to one and not another, but I've learned not to miss the hand of God in my life when the outcome of circumstances is obviously a "God thing." The woman in the story below has learned that lesson, as well.

"You really shouldn't stand around in places like this without watching your back."

Holly Hudson froze, then slowly turned to her right. A man had silently walked up behind her and stood just inches away. His dark clothing matched his short black hair; his steady brown eyes seemed to pierce her soul. She stared at the horizontal scar that scored his left cheek.

"You don't know where you are, do you?" he asked, breaking the silence. His tone made the comment more of a statement than a question. "People get killed here all the time," he said, gesturing to the area underneath the west end of Portland's Burnside Bridge. Holly had sought refuge under the bridge during an Oregon rainstorm while she waited for a ride home. "There's all kinds of heroin addicts around. Just last week, somebody got stabbed here."

Holly shivered. "I had no idea," she said. "I figured it's safe enough. They have outdoor markets here on the weekends. And it's still light out."

"On the *weekends* it's safe," he corrected her. "*Not* during the week!"

Holly's heart began racing as the man continued his rebuke. "You should be standing at the light-rail station over there. You stick out like a sore thumb."

"I was going to take the MAX all the way home, but it's not running," she explained. "They closed it down because of some kind of police action on the other side of the river. We had to get off. So I called my boyfriend and asked him to come get me."

"How long will that be?"

"About twenty minutes. It's been ten minutes already. Should I move over that way?" Holly glanced toward some nearby shops.

"No, you should be okay," the man replied. "They know me around here, and they see me talking to you. But I'll keep an eye on you just in case." The man turned and strode across the street toward the Willamette River, instantly blending with the scattered people loitering in the area.

Holly swallowed, watching his every move. Who were "they" who knew this man? Then she looked—really looked—at the area where she had chosen to wait for her ride.

He was right. She didn't know where she was.

The people wandering under the bridge where she stood and those hanging around across the street wore ripped, disheveled clothing and had unkempt hair. Some had sunken, hungry eyes. And as soon as the man in black walked away from her, several of the "locals" drifted in her direction.

Trying to appear casual, Holly wandered away from the bridge and further down the street. Almost instantly, three people gathered where she had been standing, as if to point out that she had invaded their turf.

Adrenaline pumped through Holly's veins as she realized she had naively put herself in a bad position. "Lord," she whispered, "I'm scared. I can't believe I did something so foolish. Please take care of me!"

Holly felt safer in her new location, but she longed for the security of her unexpected champion. She spotted him across the street, and he came over and stood next to her again. "Did you see how they came out of the woodwork as soon as I left?" he asked.

"Oh, yes," Holly agreed. "They sure did."

"I tell you what. I'll wait with you until your friend comes," the man said. Then he grinned and stuck out his hand. "I'm Dallas. My real name is Leroy Brown, but you can call me Dallas."

"Nice to meet you, Dallas. I'm Holly," she replied, smiling as she shook his hand. "I guess the Lord sent you to be my guardian angel today."

His eyes met Holly's again. "I've heard people say that before."

Startled, Holly looked closely at Dallas. "Oh, really? When?"

"Oh, you know . . . when people get lost in this area and ask me for directions. I seem to be sort of an unofficial Portland guide."

"Well," said Holly, "I'm glad you were here today to guide me!"

She looked hard at Dallas again. The scar on his cheek—was it an old knife wound, she wondered. "Who are you?"

"That's a good question," he said. "I haven't figured that out yet."

"Do you have a job around here?"

"I've had a hundred jobs in my lifetime," he said smoothly, evading her question. "I do like to restore classic cars. If I don't get some temp work in the next week, I have a job lined up to do that."

Suddenly, Dallas gestured to a station wagon that had just passed by. "You see that station wagon?"

"Yes," she said, wondering why he had changed the subject.

"That car is going to turn right at the corner and pick up that prostitute," he said, nodding toward a young woman walking down the street in jeans and a sweatshirt. The car turned right and the girl turned left, moving to intercept the car.

Dallas's perception amazed Holly. He did know this area!

She glanced toward the bridge once more and saw Sean, her boyfriend, waiting there at last, his car pulled over to the side of the road. Dallas followed her gaze. "Oh, is your friend here?"

"That's him," she said, relieved.

"Well, let me walk you over."

They reached the car in a few seconds, but Dallas didn't stop or say good-bye. He just looked at Holly and said, "Take care." Then he walked toward the closed light-rail station.

Holly watched him for a second. Then she jumped into the car, locked the door, and looked at Sean. "That was my guardian angel!"

"What happened?" he asked, concerned.

They pulled onto the street and as Holly began her story, she looked for Dallas. He was gone.

For weeks afterward, Holly would look out the window of the

light-rail car to see if Dallas was among the street people gathered under the Burnside Bridge. She never saw him again.

> If you make the Lord your refuge, if you make the Most
> High your shelter, no evil will conquer you . . . For he
> orders his angels to protect you wherever you go
> (Psalm 91:9–11).

A PICTURE

14.

· *armed and ready* ·

Why is one person spared physical catastrophe and another is not? Close calls are all around us. Most of the time we're oblivious to the Hand that protected us from danger. And while anxious prayers for protection are not always answered . . . sometimes they are! There is a police officer in the Bay Area who certainly believes this today.

A dozen jocular and animated police officers filed into the briefing room at eleven P.M. The graveyard shift of the Newark Police Department—located in a San Francisco Bay Area working-class suburb midway between Oakland and San Jose—was about to begin.

"Listen up, guys," the staff sergeant began. "Earlier this evening an Oakland police officer made a routine stop. As he walked up to the car, a perpetrator stepped up and shot him to death with an AK-47 . . . We've got a cop killer on the loose. He fled the scene, but we were able to get a physical description and make on his car. It's all in this briefing paper," he said, as he passed copies around the room.

Newark patrolman Patrick Hunt glanced at the suspect's description.

"He is armed and dangerous," the sergeant continued. "We've been told that the perp may be in our area. Be careful out there."

The subsequent East Bay manhunt failed to locate the gunman over the next week. Seven days after their comrade had been killed in the line of duty, Patrick attended a men's Bible study with three friends from church and his younger brother, Tim, a police officer in neighboring Fremont.

Patrick was struggling with the cop killing. When the group took prayer requests, he said, "I know God exists, but I can't comprehend how He can know the thoughts and deeds of everyone. I was at an Athletic's baseball game recently and, as I looked around the Coliseum, I wondered how God could know the thoughts of all fifty thousand people. And when that officer got ambushed . . ."

Patrick didn't have to finish. His buddies knew he was wrestling with his emotions, so they prayed God would help him understand His all-powerful nature.

Several hours later Patrick reported for his graveyard shift. A light rain was falling.

At 12:40 A.M., the 911 board at the dispatch center lit up like a Christmas tree. "There's a man shooting at everyone in sight!" screamed one caller.

"A van got hit in the motel parking lot!" cried another. "Now it's trying to get out of here!"

Patrolling alone in his cruiser, Patrick was dispatched as a backup officer to the motel, located in the center of Newark. Up ahead, he spotted the disabled van—parked on the wrong side of the road. Its headlights beamed brightly through the windshield, blinding him.

Patrick slowed as he approached the van, wary that a gunman could be hiding in the shadows.

Ka-blam!

The window on the driver's side of Patrick's patrol car exploded in his face, scraping his exposed skin like a wire brush. More shots rang out. Lead fragments and door shrapnel exploded all around him. His leg suddenly burned with pain.

Instinct and police training took over. Patrick slammed the car into reverse. The windshield exploded. Bullets whizzed by as Patrick continued to floor the damaged vehicle. Then he heard two tires pop.

"God, please don't let me die!" he screamed, as the crippled car rolled on two tire rims. He backed up the bullet-riddled cruiser a quarter mile before another officer came to his aid.

The shooting stopped. Patrick pulled himself out of the car and began shaking uncontrollably.

"My God, you've been hit!" said the other officer.

Patrick looked down. Blood was seeping through his ripped pants. Within minutes, paramedics arrived on the scene. They quickly cut off Patrick's pant legs and assessed his injuries. Then they put him on a gurney and carted him off to the hospital.

Patrick's wife, Lynette, five months pregnant with their third child, met Patrick at the hospital. In the early morning hours, doctors cleaned his legs of the visible bullet fragments and lead shrapnel. Then his brother Tim arrived.

"It's the same perp who killed the Oakland officer last week," Tim reported. "He just started shooting people in the motel parking lot. One guy was on his bicycle. He survived, but it looks like he'll be paralyzed. You know the driver of that van? The van got hit, and when someone came to his aid, the suspect opened fire on the Good Samaritan and nearly tore his leg off. He played dead as the gunman stood over him and said, 'Sorry I had to shoot you, man.'"

"Did we catch him?"

"Not yet. He's running through streets, pounding on doors with the butt of his AK-47. A perimeter has been established. Anyway, if you're up to it, you're wanted down at the office. Reports have to be filed."

At the police station, Patrick and Tim heard that the suspect had carjacked a BMW. The driver and her children fled for their lives.

The perimeter tightened, and when officers surrounded the stolen car, they ordered the gunman to give up peacefully. When the suspect reached for his rifle, a hail of police gunfire brought the night of terror to an end.

Patrick realized how terrifying the previous night had been when he visited the crime scene later that morning. He stepped out and surveyed the area where his patrol car was first hit. He found ten bullet casings. The first pile of spent casings lay no farther than twenty feet from where his car had been, and other casings moved closer with each shot.

"He had a flash suppresser on the gun," said another officer. "That's why you never saw him. It's amazing that you weren't killed at such close range."

Then Patrick inspected his damaged patrol car. Two bullet holes had punched right through the center of the driver's door. Had they not been deflected, or if one bullet had traveled an inch and a half higher, he would have been struck in the opening between the front and back of his bullet-proof vest. One round was lodged in the portable radio on his left hip.

As for the flying bullets that never found their mark—Patrick realized he should have been dead. Any doubts of God's almighty power were erased. God had answered his hasty prayer and protected him.

> Though I am surrounded by troubles, you will
> preserve me against the anger of
> my enemies (Psalm 138:7).

A PORTRAIT

15.

· *down to the wire* ·

Immediate answers to prayer. You want them. I want them. But God simply does not always work that way. And to get His best, we must be patient. In some cases, we must wait until the last minute for His answer to come. And when the clock shows 11:59, get ready to be amazed. The woman below certainly was.

The infant arrived at the door in a gunny sack, carried by a Madras (now Chennai), India, utility worker who found her on the street, abandoned, naked, and near death. Colleen Redit took her in, notwithstanding the fact there already were thirteen girls in her legally adopted family. When the baby, whom Colleen named Judith, miraculously survived through prayer, intravenous feedings, and blood transfusions, she became number fourteen.

Since her arrival in India more than thirty-five years ago, Colleen has given her heart and opened her home to thousands of girls and young women. First, she longed to tell them about Jesus, but the missionary from New Zealand also searched for a way to lift their self-esteem and build a measure of independence.

Most of the teenagers Colleen met on the hard streets of Madras had finished school but had virtually no chance to escape dire poverty apart from an arranged marriage, which might tie a girl to a man as old as her father.

One day, Colleen moved the car out of the garage of her rented home, wiped the oil off the floor, and invited girls to learn how to cross-stitch, knit, and type. Girls flocked to the garage, and Colleen looked for larger premises. In the meantime, she registered her work with the government, calling it the Christian Mission Charitable Trust.

Colleen and the girls were invited to sell their handicrafts at various churches in the region. Colleen found a larger building to rent—one with enough room to start a hostel and orphanage for girls like Judith. By day, the girls used every available inch to produce crafts; at night, they moved furniture and equipment to open a place to sleep. Colleen wondered how much longer they would be able to stay at 18 Khader Nawaz Khan Road in Madras.

One evening in 1994, Colleen received a phone call from an acquaintance who offered to sell her a piece of land.

"But I don't have any money to pay for it," she said.

"I still want you to come look it over," the vendor replied. "Can you join me at the property this Sunday afternoon?"

Colleen shrugged her shoulders and agreed. What she saw was a ramshackle two-story building ready for the demolition ball.

"What I'm offering you is the land," said the man. "The building will have to be torn down."

"But where am I going to put my girls?" Colleen asked.

"Tell me a little about your work."

Colleen described the work of the Christian Mission Charitable Trust, but the man also wanted to know where the financial support came from and who paid Colleen's salary.

"I have been called by God to His work," she said. "I look to Him day by day, and He has never failed me."

"Yes, I see. Well, here's my offer. My original asking price was thirty-eight lakhs per ground," he said, using an Indian form of measurement, "but for you, I am happy to reduce the price to twenty-eight lakhs per ground."

"I was thinking of something along the lines of twenty-seven lakhs per ground," Colleen replied.

"Okay," he said. "We have a deal."

"Before we have a deal, I must pray and seek the mind of the Lord, and I will need a month for an answer."

"A month? Sure, that's okay. I will take the property off the market until you decide. You have my word."

During the month, a friend from Singapore called and asked Colleen if he could bring a small team of men to visit the mission. The men were impressed with the impact being made in the lives of young women. When they commented on the overcrowded living conditions, Colleen asked if they would like to see a derelict building that the mission was thinking of purchasing.

That evening, they gathered around the building and prayed for the Lord's guidance. Then the men boarded a return flight to Singapore.

Meanwhile, Colleen continued to pray. Monday was the last day of the one-month deadline, and Colleen knew she had to phone the vendor and tell him that she could not complete the purchase.

Colleen was sitting at her desk Monday morning when the fax machine gushed paper. She leaned over and began reading. The men in Singapore had discussed the mission's need with church elders, who decided to allot $40,000 (in Singapore dollars) to the Christian Mission Charitable Trust.

Colleen stared at the fax, wondering if she could believe her eyes. Then she locked her office door, turned off the light, and thanked God for this clear and direct answer to her prayers.

She called the vendor to tell him she could proceed with the property purchase.

"Good," he replied. "I almost called you last night to inquire about the status of our transaction, but something held me back."

"If you had called, I would have told you to go ahead without us, because I had no leading from the Lord," Colleen said.

"It's good you didn't—I have been inundated with offers at the original asking price!"

A gleaming, six-story structure opened its doors in Chennai (formerly Madras) in 1999. Today, the structure educates and feeds more than 600 destitute children and young people.

"Keep on asking, and you will be given what you ask for.
Keep on looking, and you will find. Keep on knocking,
and the door will be opened" (Matthew 7:7).

A PORTRAIT

16.

· *back home at last* ·

Some people have experienced so much pain—both physical and emotional—that it makes it hard for them to see God. The Bible verse they most relate to is Jesus' statement, "Here on earth you will have many trials . . ." Though they may not know the verse, they know trials! Yet our lot in life is not to be a pawn in the hand of a fickle "God" who doles out trouble on unsuspecting victims. Jesus' statement is simply a fact. The second half to that verse, however, is a promise: ". . . but be of good cheer. I have overcome the world." If there ever was a story that illustrates this passage, this one is it!

William George Loney, a harsh man who ruled his family with an iron fist as his Irish forefathers had before him, never gave his blessing when his daughter was courted by the eligible young men of Portadown. *Nobody will ever be good enough for my Sarah,* he thought.

Sarah chafed at his restrictions, but what options did a lass have in the late 1930s, when war clouds were darkening skies over Europe? She and her father had terrible rows, pushing Sarah to search for love in the arms of other men. One of those liaisons resulted in the birth of a daughter, May, when Sarah was twenty years old. May was handed to "aunties" to rear.

Sarah fell in love with another bloke, and while Nazi Messerschmidts pummeled England in 1940, a son, named Jim, was born.

Scorned by the Portadown townspeople, Sarah went "in service"—walking to people's houses early in the morning to scrub floors, wash clothes and dishes, change beds, and perform other menial tasks. Though Sarah had grown up in a Protestant family, a big-hearted Catholic lady offered to look after Jim during the day.

But Sarah could not soldier on. Working her fingers to the bone for a pound note or two and trying to raise a toddler—and visit May as often as possible—proved too formidable a task. With great sorrow, Sarah decided to give up Jim for adoption.

The Patterson family lived thirty-five miles away in Ballygawley. They knew Sarah and offered to adopt Jim. William and Edith Patterson drove to Portadown and brought Jim back to their home.

Three-year-old Jim loved his new father and imitated everything he did on the farm, from mucking stalls to milking cows.

Twice a year, relatives looked in on him, including Aunt Sally, who walked peculiarly, swaying left and right.

"Why does Aunt Sally walk like a penguin?" Jim asked one day.

"She has rheumatism," his adoptive mother said.

William Patterson died suddenly when Jim was twelve, the cause of death listed as septic poisoning that started with a finger cut. Edith would not allow Jim to see his father at the hospital or attend the funeral. She was angry at God, angry at the world, and angry at Jim, her nearest target. For nearly a year, she stripped Jim and whipped him with a sally rod.

"Your mother was nothing but a whore," she screamed, as the rod came down. "You are nothing but a little bastard."

As Jim reached his teen years, Edith verbally abused him. "I give up!" she yelled one afternoon. "Your father's gone, and I can't do anything with you. I should just take you to the police station and let them lock you up."

Jim, seventeen at the time, thought she meant it. He hatched a plan to run away from home and live with one of his adoptive sisters, Mary Barnett, who was living in the Midlands north of London. Jim had never been out of Tyrone County, let alone Ireland. Somehow, he managed to take a train and find his sister.

After working for a time in a biscuit factory, Jim joined the British Army—the Royal Engineer's Regiment at Aldershot in Hampshire. He met a young woman, fell in love, and became engaged. Then he learned that she had been unfaithful, which stirred up all the old feelings of abandonment and betrayal.

Jim had once read that a man could live forty days without food, eight days without water, and up to six minutes without oxygen—but only seconds without hope. He made plans to take his life. After pouring a tall whiskey, he washed down one hundred sleeping tablets, and then lay down to die.

Jim awakened the next morning in the army sick bay. A few days after his suicide attempt, he was nursing a drink at a bar when John, a member of the parachute regiment, took a seat next to him.

They began talking, and Jim poured out his woeful story. "Do I have any hope?" he asked.

"Yes, you do," John said, "the hope of Jesus Christ."

John laid out the story of the gospel, and Jim said he wanted to give his life to Christ.

"Do you want to pray with me?" John asked.

"Right here in the bar? Are you kidding?"

"Okay," said John. "I know a church nearby."

At eleven P.M., they walked into an empty Anglican church, and Jim found the hope, peace, and joy he had been searching so long for. "Oh, God, if you can heal my broken heart and dry my tears and give me hope, I'll go to the nations of the world to tell them of the hope you have given me."

Life improved in a hurry. Jim met Christine, and they married on August 27, 1960.

During their honeymoon, the couple returned to Northern Ireland to visit relatives, including Jim's older adoptive sister, Jean Davidson, who lived in Portadown.

During their visit, Jean asked, "Have you ever thought about your real mother?"

"Yes, I have," Jim answered. "But I don't know my mother. I don't know whether she is dead or alive."

"Oh, your mum is very much alive, and you know her."

"What are you talking about?"

"Do you remember Aunt Sally?" Jean said, as she showed him an old black-and-white photo of the woman who used to visit the farm when he was a boy.

"You mean the one who walked like a penguin?"

"Yes. That's your mum."

The world stopped for Jim.

"She knows you're married," Jean continued. "You can see her if you like, but it's up to you."

"When?"

"Today at three o'clock."

"That's less than an hour! Where is she?"

Jean stood and walked over to the large picture window. "See the second house just past the corner? That's where your mum lives."

A few minutes before three, Jim and Christine began their walk down the street. Jim immediately recognized the woman walking toward them—her stiff-legged penguin gait gave her away.

They met at a crossroads and fell into each other's arms. Sarah Loney was crying hysterically.

"It's okay, Mum," Jim said, holding her as tight as he could.

Sarah stepped back and attempted to speak. "On this very spot on the road seventeen years ago, I handed you to the Pattersons. To be reunited at the very place . . ." Sarah composed herself. "I thank God for this day."

Jim learned that his mother had become a Christian and had eventually married, and all that time she was praying that God would save her son and use him in the ministry. Three years after being reunited with his mother, Jim entered seminary.

A decade later, Jim returned to Northern Ireland to pastor a church fifteen miles from Portadown. Today, he is pastor of Elim Church in East Finchley, North London, confident that God had a special plan for his life all along.

And we know that God causes everything to work
together for the good of those who love God and are
called according to his purpose for them (Romans 8:28).

A PICTURE

17.

· *a heart to save* ·

Do you ever wonder if you should ask God for a miracle? Stop wondering! The God of the Bible loves to perform miracles if they are in line with His perfect will. But first we must ask. Second, we must not doubt that He is able. Why? Because He IS able!

"Dr. Meeker, please report immediately to the ICU."

Meg Meeker, senior pediatric resident at Children's Hospital in Milwaukee, Wisconsin, had a feeling that the monotonic summons over the intercom was not good news. Then again, if she had learned anything about the medical profession, it was that being paged to the pediatric intensive care unit was never good news.

Dr. Meeker strode into the ICU and saw a half-dozen gowned colleagues gathered around a small bed.

"It's Katie," said a nurse. "We have a code blue. She's not responding."

Meg looked at the cardiac monitor. The rapidly sinking blood pressure told her what everyone else in the room already knew about the six-month-old infant: Katie's heart was giving out. She was dying.

Dr. Meeker's colleagues stood aside so that she could begin efforts to restart the heart. She took two small electric pads in her hands and attempted to restart the life-giving muscle. The baby's body heaved with the first jolt of electricity, but the heart failed to start beating.

"Dr. Meeker, her father is here."

Meg turned around and saw a distraught father standing in the doorway. "We can't let him see this," she whispered to another resident. "Too traumatic. Ask him to take a seat in the waiting room."

Meg turned her attention back to Katie. She went by the book as she fought to bring Katie back to life, but the infant did not respond to her ministrations. Katie was at death's door as her pallor turned from blue to white to a brownish gray. Meg knew that if the blood flow to the brain stopped for much longer, the girl would be severely brain damaged.

Lord, what should I do? Meg was the senior medical technician in the room, and everyone was looking for her to come up with an answer.

"Listen up, everybody. Our only hope is internal cardiac massage, but before we begin, we need to pray. Lord," she began, "we ask that you spare the life of this girl. Please help us to start her heart again."

There wasn't much time. She picked up a pair of oversized cutting shears and cut into Katie's chest to split it open. Then she reached under the chest cavity with her left hand and found Katie's heart. She began squeezing it, causing the muscle to send much-needed blood to and from the heart. As Meg continued pinching the heart, the monitor reported that Katie's blood pressure was mounting. Pink color returned to her skin.

"She's alive!" Dr. Meeker cried out.

Katie was stabilized, and a pediatric cardiac surgeon was called in to attend to further cardiac complications. While Katie was being attended to, Meg walked into the waiting room.

Hospital protocol did not allow Meg to speak to the parents; that duty was reserved for the primary care physician. Meg noticed the couple was sobbing, and it took every ounce of strength not to walk over and tell them that their daughter was going to make it.

When she turned a corner, Meg stopped and leaned against the wall. *Lord, thank you for guiding my hand, but I pray that you*

*would somehow make it known to those parents that you intervened
and saved that little girl's life.*

Meg found a phone to call her husband, Walt. After telling
him what happened, she said, "God literally walked into the
room and held my hand as I opened that baby's chest."

"No, you're wrong," Walt replied. "Jesus was in that room before you came in."

> If you need wisdom—if you want to know what
> God wants you to do—ask him, and he will
> gladly tell you (James 1:5).

A PORTRAIT

18.

· *nothing was wasted* ·

The death of a loved one rarely seems to make sense, no matter what the age or circumstances. And for the first few years after a death, the nerves of loved ones are often too raw to find purpose amid the pain. Sometimes on this earth, however, we get a glimpse of what God has done. His big portrait comes into view, and all we can say is "Now I see."

"Come give Daddy a hug."

Seven-year-old Diane Morris put on her bravest face and then wrapped her tiny arms around the hunched-over frame of her father, Bernard. Dressed in a well-creased brown U.S. Army uniform topped with a hard-bill cap, Bernard tousled Diane's hair as they both fought back tears. The car horn beeped a second time. With a sweep of his hand, Bernard waved good-bye to Diane, her ten-year-old sister, Charlene, and her little brother, Tommy, who was four.

The year was 1944, and Uncle Sam's draft notice had informed Bernard he was now the property of the U.S. Army. The timing couldn't have been worse. His wife, Alene, was quarantined in a tuberculosis hospital. The only way to keep the three kids together under the same roof was to place them with foster parents who lived twenty-five miles from their home in Oxnard, California.

"What if he doesn't come back?" Diane asked Charlene as their father disappeared down the street.

"Oh, he will."

"But what if he doesn't?"

Her question hung in the air. Over the next few months, their father wrote as often as he could, but censors stripped out any pertinent information. One sentence was particularly revealing, however: *Tell Aunt Phyllis that I'll be seeing her soon.*

Diane knew she didn't have an "Aunt Phyllis" in the family. Then she heard adults say her father was trying to tell them he was on his way to the Philippines. All she knew was that her father went somewhere overseas to fight in a terrible war.

One afternoon, Diane was summoned from class at school. When she saw her mother, Diane knew something was wrong. Alene's face was ashen gray. Her hand clutched a telegram: THE SECRETARY OF WAR DESIRES ME TO EXPRESS HIS DEEP REGRET THAT YOUR HUSBAND, PRIVATE BERNARD L. MORRIS, HAS BEEN REPORTED

MISSING IN ACTION SINCE 11 FEBRUARY IN SOUTHWEST PACIFIC AREA. J. A. ULIO, ADJUTANT GENERAL.

"What does it mean, Mommy?"

"It means Daddy's probably dead."

Alene Morris had learned from other service families that the armed forces followed a two-step protocol when a body was not found. Six torturous months passed before the second telegram arrived in September 1945—more than a month after war in the Pacific ended. The telegram stated that Private Morris had been killed in action and UNAVOIDABLE CIRCUMSTANCES MADE NECESSARY THE UNUSUAL LAPSE OF TIME IN REPORTING YOUR HUSBAND'S DEATH TO YOU. A followup letter to Mrs. Morris filled in the details:

> On 6 February 1945, your husband sailed from Hollandia, Dutch New Guinea, for the Philippine Islands. On the morning of 11 February at approximately nine o'clock, his ship was attacked by an enemy submarine and received two torpedo hits amidships. The explosion broke the vessel in half and the entire stern section sank in a matter of minutes, trapping everyone inside.
>
> During an extensive search, all survivors were rescued by two Navy ships in the convoy. I deeply regret that your husband was not among the survivors. Death would have come

very quickly, and I am sure he could have suffered very little, if
any, pain.

　Private Morris died that our people might continue to live
in freedom and, in that great ideal, may you find solace.
　Ralph C. Moor
　Major, U.S. Army

With Alene quarantined again in a tuberculosis hospital, the
family decided not to arrange a funeral or memorial service. Besides, the body was never recovered. Not having had a chance to
say good-bye to her father left a gaping hole in Diane's heart.

Alene Morris's health eventually improved to the point that she
was able to move back to Oxnard with the three children. Diane
suddenly became very ill with acute nephritis, a kidney infection.
She spent the next three months in the hospital.

　Meanwhile, life presented one challenge after another for Diane's mother. Raising three children on a pension was proving to
be more than she could handle. Alene turned to drink when
Charlene and Diane were old enough to care for Tommy.

　Aware of the difficulties, the pastor of a neighborhood church
where the children had attended Sunday school offered Charlene and Diane a scholarship to attend summer camp. There Di-

ane, thirteen years old, made the decision to trust Jesus Christ with her life.

GI Bill benefits and a scholarship for "war orphans" enabled Diane to attend the University of California at Santa Barbara. She had no trouble declaring a major. Diane had wanted to teach primary school since she was a little girl. At her college graduation, her junior high music teacher, Marge Brown, appeared with her husband, Larry.

"What are you doing here?" Diane exclaimed after the cap-and-gown ceremony.

"To watch you graduate," Marge replied. "We wouldn't miss this day for the world."

Marge and Larry Brown had taken Diane under their wings years ago, but now they had important news.

"We're leaving soon," Marge began.

"Where are you going?"

"To Taiwan to teach at a school for missionary kids. That's where we believe the Lord is leading us. We're going with a mission called Overseas Crusades."

A seed was planted in her heart that afternoon. Diane spent the next two years teaching in the Los Angeles County public school system, but newsletters from the Browns in Taiwan and prayer for their ministry nurtured a desire to teach at a mission school. At a holiday Christian conference, Diane prayerfully considered what she felt God wanted her to do with her life.

Lord, I'm willing to go anywhere for you.

Certain of her calling to teach mission kids, she told her school district she would not be returning in the fall. Then she wrote to Overseas Crusades (now known as OC International) and asked what she should do next. It was suggested that Diane attend a one-year graduate program at Multnomah Biblical Seminary in Portland, Oregon. With no money in savings, Diane saw God working again when she learned that the same GI Bill that provided for her college education would also pay for graduate school.

That year at Multnomah, a man came on campus, asking to see Diane. His wife had been Diane's Pioneer Girls leader. During their visit in the dining hall, he said that if Diane wanted to go overseas, then he and his wife would like to help in her financial support.

Finally, Diane was ready for the field. She thought she was headed for Taiwan, but at the last minute, she was placed at Faith Academy, a missionary school on the outskirts of Manila.

Shortly after her arrival in the Philippines, Diane went with missionary friends on a Sunday drive. They stopped at the Filipino-American War Memorial for those killed in World War II.

"My father was killed in the war," she told her hosts. Terrible memories came rushing back to her. The constant fear of not knowing, the fateful letters, and the years longing for a daddy to hold, all rushed back into her heart like a flood.

The memorial consisted of well-tended lawns dotted with tens of thousands of white crosses. Diane and her friends strolled over to a large, semicircular wall with inscribed panels whose heading was: COMRADES IN ARMS WHOSE EARTHLY RESTING PLACE IS KNOWN ONLY TO GOD.

Under the then-forty-eight states, the names were arranged alphabetically and by rank and date of service.

Was his name there?

"California," she said as she scanned the list, her hands trembling. There it was: MORRIS, BERNARD LEE, PRIVATE.

Diane nearly collapsed in tears as friends wrapped their arms around her. "There was no body, no funeral, no ceremony," she said. "All we got was a telegram and a Purple Heart. For years, my sister and I discussed the stories we heard about people who were thought to be dead in the war, who suddenly appeared on the doorstep . . ."

God had worked nearly twenty years in her life to bring her to this place outside Manila, on this day, to provide closure for her father's death. Living in a foster home had prepared her for what the mission kids who boarded at Faith Academy were going through. Her father's tragic death had funded her college education. Then God sent her to the very part of the world where her father had died. A perfect circle!

Then Diane remembered a line from missionary Amy Carmichael's biography: "God never wastes his servant's time."

Diane Morris taught twenty-eight years at Faith Academy in the Philippines. She now serves as the Coordinator for Missionary Kids and Families at OC International's headquarters in Colorado Springs, Colorado.

Pure and lasting religion in the sight of God our
Father means that we must care for orphans and
widows in their troubles, and refuse to let the
world corrupt us (James 1:27).

A PORTRAIT

19.

· *the teddy bear* ·

Sometimes, for God to break through the hard heart of a certain person, He must reveal Himself in remarkable ways known only to that person. As He does that, He will typically ask His followers to do things that don't appear to make sense. God is not limited to our human, finite wisdom in healing deep emotional wounds as an angry bear of a man discovered . . .

Earl's crossed arms and permanent grimace told everyone in the room he didn't want to be there. Meanwhile, Kim wiped tears away as she expressed her desire for a happy marriage with a husband who managed his anger.

The couple was attending a Cleansing Stream seminar, led by Church on the Way in Van Nuys, California. Earl, sporting a two-day stubble on his chin, was a bear of a guy—an angry, burly man with an intimidating scowl. His demure wife, Kim, radiated warmth.

During a portion of the seminar held at a hotel, Earl and Kim joined three other couples, including Mike and Judith Hayes, for informal counseling and prayer. Judith, part of Cleansing Stream's leadership team, began with routine questions: "Where did you meet? How long have you been married? What do you do for a living?"

Earl grunted a few answers in between complaints about this "inquisition," but Judith, who believes the Lord has given her the biblical spiritual gift of discernment, could see right through his bravado. Something was bothering this guy.

Kim said that if Earl did not get help soon, she saw no way the marriage could continue. Years of belligerence and yelling had taken their toll.

The session concluded with a time of prayer. With her eyes closed, Judith kept seeing a fuzzy brown teddy bear with a plaid bow around its neck. She wondered if she hadn't received enough sleep the previous night. What did a teddy bear have to do with this guy?

As the meeting broke up for lunch, a leader asked if Earl felt any differently. "I never believed in any of this anyway, so the answer is no," he replied. "I only did this for my wife."

Judith leaned to Mike and said, "I know this sounds crazy, but the Lord wants me to buy Earl a teddy bear."

Mike rolled his eyes, but after twenty-nine years of marriage, he had learned his wife's spiritual antennae usually captured the right signal. "Okay, let's go find one."

At a nearby market, which happened to be having a sale on teddy bears, Judith found the exact one she envisioned: a furry brown bear with a plaid bow. She purchased one and wrote a note explaining that God had told her to give Earl this bear, although she didn't know why.

When the seminar regrouped in the hotel ballroom, Judith found Earl and Kim sitting toward the back. She walked over and handed him a brown paper bag. When he lifted the bear out of the bag, Earl clutched it to his chest and his shoulders began heaving uncontrollably. Tears rolled down his cheeks. People couldn't help looking his way.

After pulling him aside for a few minutes, seminar leaders asked Earl to approach the front of the room, which he did, clutching Kim and his teddy bear.

"I would like to thank the group for praying for me," he stammered. "Something happened here today, and it happened because a lady brought me this teddy bear.

"You see, no one in the whole wide world knows what this teddy bear means to me. When I was a little boy, I had a very authoritarian father, and he regularly beat me. One day I disobeyed him and, for my punishment, he took me and my favorite teddy bear to the backyard incinerator, where he burned my teddy bear right before my eyes. I was so crushed, so hurt, that I never forgave him. I realize today that God knew my unforgivingness caused great anger in my marriage. Now that God gave me back my teddy bear, I can start healing."

Dabbing at tears, Judith sat in awe of God's tender grace and unfailing love.

The unfailing love of the Lord never ends! By his
mercies we have been kept from complete destruction.
Great is his faithfulness; his mercies begin afresh
each day (Lamentations 3:22–23).

A PICTURE

20.

· on the heels of an angel ·

While accidents and bad things happen to innocent people, there is no doubting the fact that God holds children in high regard. His angels protect our loved ones in countless ways through miracles we never see. After raising four boys, I can honestly say it's amazing that any child arrives at adulthood without trauma and harm. The story below illustrates why children are so well protected.

Doris ran straight toward the McKenzie River, hoping and praying Roger hadn't reached it yet. A three-year-old would be no match for the cold, roaring water.

The Smallings lived in a log cabin deep in the woods behind a relative's riverfront property near Springfield, Oregon. Doris arrived home to find Roger's baby-sitter, Jennie, asleep on the sofa.

"Where's Roger?"

Startled, Jennie jumped up.

"Uh-oh, I must have dozed. He was here a minute ago, playing right beside me."

"How do you know how long it was if you were asleep?" Doris said. "We've got to find him. Run over to your house and see if he's with your little brother Ned. I'll head toward the river. If you find him, come yelling."

Doris ran to the yard to check Puppy's enclosure. Roger loved the German shepherd his grandfather had given him and promptly named him Puppy. Long after the ball of fur had grown larger than the boy, the name stuck.

Puppy wasn't there. Knowing how much Roger loved to show the "ribber" to Puppy, Doris ran straight toward the McKenzie, dodging pine branches.

God, I worried when Auntie offered this log cabin next to the river . . . Dear God, you love that little boy, too, and you know he's my life. Put your protecting arms around him. Please!

Like giant cymbals that crashed without pause, the sound of the cold and wild McKenzie cascading over the rocks swallowed Doris's frantic calls for "Ro-ger! Ro-ger!" She didn't see the tree root that stretched across the path and caught her foot, slamming her face down in the dirt.

Please don't let my ankle be broken. I've got to find my little boy. Please, God, help us.

Doris grabbed an overhanging branch. After pulling herself to a standing position, she shifted her weight to the injured foot. A twinge flashed through her ankle, but she could walk.

Point me in the right direction, God.

Doris staggered toward the water's edge. "Ro-ger!" she frantically yelled ever louder above the river's roar.

Was that a dog's bark? It seemed to come from the river straight ahead. *Please let it be Puppy. Let my son be okay.*

A bright shaft of sunlight spotlighted Roger's golden curls. The toddler was standing on a fallen tree jutting out into the river, about ten feet from shore, with Puppy beside him. If her son lost his balance and tumbled into the river, Doris doubted she could save him. She gasped when Puppy barked and Roger looked up, fixing his gaze straight ahead. The last thing she wanted was for Roger to see her and make any fast movements.

Suddenly, the boy hunched down on all fours and started crawling toward shore. Puppy hunched down as well, almost groveling as he crawled behind Roger.

Doris felt transfixed as she quietly watched Roger inch his way to the bank. She held her breath, wondering if the rough bark was cutting his knees.

Help him, Lord Jesus. Help him keep his mind only on the crawling. We can fix his knees. Bring him to me, Lord, please.

The boy and his dog didn't waver or change pace, creeping along the trunk. Just before they reached the bank, Puppy straightened and leaped over Roger, barking and running toward Doris. Roger stood and ran the last few feet into his mother's arms.

Doris hugged Roger so hard he squealed.

"Rogie, I was so scared. I prayed Jesus would take care of you, and he did. Now I want to hold you while I thank him."

"Mommy," he interrupted, wiggling out of her grasp, "that man was so nice. He told me and Puppy to get down on our knees."

"What man?"

"Didn't you see him? He told me to crawl like you're smelling the log. 'Don't look at anything but my heels and don't stop till I tell you to stand up.' And you know what, Mommy? Even Puppy knew what he said."

Who was that man? Doris wondered. Roger had a great imagination, but this was something else.

When Doris examined Roger's knees—not a blemish on either one—she finally understood. God had sent a guardian angel to protect her son.

For the angel of the Lord guards all who fear him,
and he rescues them (Psalm 34:7).

A PORTRAIT

21.

· *father's day* ·

A hole in the heart is never quite so big as when a father's love is missed. Like our innate need to know the God who loves us, our need for a father never goes away. Though death and divorce have made many children "fatherless," God promises that He will be especially close to these hurting souls. The key: recognizing that God is the loving father you always needed.

Single-parent families were not common in the 1950s, especially in the predominantly Catholic community of Niles, Ohio, where Velma Meares grew up. Kids as well as adults often inquired where her dad worked or where he was.

"He's dead," Velma replied, never getting used to saying those words. When people reacted with shock, Velma felt even more uncomfortable.

In Velma's first-grader's mind, every problem was linked to her father's death—he had had a heart attack when she was four years old. *If only I had a dad, everything would be all right,* she thought. Every night in bed she would lie in the dark and pretend that her dad was sitting next to her. Velma would tell him how much she missed him and whatever else was on her mind. She knew her father wasn't there, but, after a while, she began to feel that Someone really was listening.

Velma's mother had been an alcoholic like her father, and, about a year before he died, she persuaded him to go with her to Alcoholics Anonymous. In this particular group, members acknowledged that to stop drinking, they totally depended on God, not just on AA or their own willpower. After the first meeting, Velma's mother never touched alcohol again.

To make ends meet, the widow with four children worked two or three jobs, sometimes on Sundays. One of her co-workers offered to take the children to church. There Velma realized God was the one overhearing her bedtime conversations. She stopped pretending to talk to her dad and began praying to her *heavenly* Father. As time went by, her mother went to church with the kids on the Sundays she wasn't working.

When she was seven years old, Velma experienced bouts of insomnia and began praying that she would be able to go right to sleep. After several nights, God spoke gently to her heart. "Don't you trust me? I love you. I know you're afraid. You don't need to ask me over and over every night."

During summer camp meetings when she was eleven, Velma trusted Jesus as her Savior. As the evangelist spoke, Velma's heart pounded. She wanted to be sure she would go to heaven, because she had learned that her dad had given his heart to the Lord in the hospital before he died. She wanted to make sure she saw him again.

After graduating from high school, when Velma was asked to teach a preschool Sunday school class, she realized she had just been going through the motions of being a Christian for quite a while. To teach children about Jesus, she knew she needed to be closer to Him herself. So Velma made a new commitment to Christ. This gave her a hunger to spend much more time reading the Bible and praying.

College followed when Velma was twenty-one. During her sophomore year at Southern California College, Velma met Dan Meares. When she married Dan, Velma was given not only a husband but also a father—Bob Meares, her father-in-law. Finally Velma could celebrate Father's Day and talk about "my dad" as her friends had for all those years.

Shortly after their honeymoon, Dan and Velma invited Dad to spend a long weekend with them—he lived a few hours away in California's Central Valley. When Bob appeared on the doorstep, Velma hugged him tightly and kissed his cheek. She could tell from the look on his face that her father-in-law was not used to hugs and kisses. Dan later told her that his grandmother died when Bob was thirteen, leaving him to be shuttled from relative to relative.

After learning more about Bob's background, Velma decided just to go for it whenever she saw him. It wasn't long before he was initiating the hugs, telling everyone within earshot that he was as pleased to have a daughter as Velma was to have a father. She had to be careful whenever walking through a mall with him. If she casually mentioned she liked "that blouse in the window," he would return later and purchase it as a gift. He loved surprising her.

During his last visit for Christmas in 1992, he had a cold. The cold developed into pneumonia. Before anyone was aware of how sick he was, he died.

Velma felt an emptiness worse than before. Once again, all she could think was *I don't have a dad.* But in the midst of her grief, once again, her *heavenly Father* heard her cry and spoke to her heart, this time during a choir rehearsal.

The choir director's family, including his daughter, was visiting the rehearsal. Watching the father/daughter relationship reminded Velma all over again of her loss.

Then the choir began singing "He Is the Same":

He is the same yesterday, today and forever
His unchanging love is forever

God used the song to remind her that He was her heavenly Father when she was a little girl and was still her Father today.

> Father to the fatherless, defender of widows—this
> is God, whose dwelling is holy. God sets the
> lonely in families (Psalm 68:5–6).

A PORTRAIT

22.

· *waiting in the wings* ·

"One person's garbage is another person's treasure." This is a true statement but tough to swallow when it refers to children. Yet we all know of couples who would like to have kids and can't—and couples who shouldn't have kids but do. Where's the justice? Well, sometimes it's in the loving, the praying, and the all-out attempt to fulfill the heart's desire to love a child and be a family.

David Clausen hadn't yet popped the question, but he was making no effort to hide his intentions.

"I want to grow old and gray with you," he said, and then he broke out in a song: "Will you still need me . . . when I'm sixty-four?"

Ginger laughed—the Beatles' Paul McCartney had nothing to worry about.

"I see a future for us, a future with a lot of kids running around," David continued, getting mushier by the minute.

Ginger loved David and knew he was serious. Should she tell him?

"David, there's just one thing."

"What would that be?"

Ginger looked away, and then said, "My system doesn't work right."

"Your system?"

"I don't get periods," she explained. "I can't have kids."

If that news bothered David, his face didn't betray him. He took a deep breath. "That's okay, Ginger. If God wants us to have kids, He'll let us. If not, then we can adopt."

Within a year, the couple stood before family and friends and pledged their love for each other. A month after the honeymoon, Ginger's mother knocked on their apartment door. "Here," she grinned, handing over a bag of baby clothes. "When are you going to make me a grandmother?"

"Oh, Mother, you know I'm not sure I can even have kids."

"You think I'm kidding? Sure, you'll have kids. Doctors have all sorts of ways to help couples these days."

"Mom, we're still on our honeymoon."

A year into the marriage, the Clausens started down a path of doctor visits, fertility drugs, and monthly pregnancy tests—all negative.

One evening, Ginger saw a television special about a couple who adopted a dozen kids, including some who had been foster kids in their home.

Adoption was out of the question—friends had told them that adoptions cost $5,000 to $10,000 or more. They didn't have that kind of money. But what about foster care? Could caring for youngsters who needed a home ease the ache in her heart?

After two years of futility with fertility drugs, Ginger carefully broached the subject with David. "What would you think about becoming foster parents?" she asked one evening. "If we can't have children, at least we could love some kids who desperately need love."

"I think we should check into it," David said, speaking without hesitation. "My only concern is that you could have your heart broken when the kids leave us."

The Clausens filled out applications, welcomed social workers into their home, and endured comprehensive interviews. They were told that they could probably expect to care for toddlers and preschoolers—kids two to five years old.

A month later Ginger received a phone call.

"Would you be willing to pick up a little boy tomorrow at the hospital?"

"What did they do to him?" Ginger asked, fearing that the child had been abused.

"He was just born," said the social worker. "You can pick him up tomorrow at ten A.M."

Ginger called her parents and several friends in their couples' Bible study. David borrowed a truck and picked up a crib, bassinet, swing, huge bag of clothing, crib sheets, and blankets. By eleven P.M., they had a bona fide nursery!

The next day, Ginger and David drove to the hospital. "We have to give him a name," she said. "I'm not going to call him Baby Boy for the rest of his life."

They finally settled on Joey—a compromise between Joseph and Joel.

"Here you go," said the social worker, handing over a six-day-old baby boy. "Good luck. He's a drug baby, you know."

"Oh, really?"

"Yes. His mother was high when she came here. Right after she gave birth, she split."

For the first week, Ginger felt she was baby-sitting a poor child all alone in the world. When her case worker failed to call for a month, she thought, *Nobody cares about this baby except us.*

As they raised Joey, the Clausens began thinking about adopting him, even though everyone had told them it would be a miracle. Young, childless parents rarely received a newborn in the first place, because they easily bonded with the infant, which complicated matters if the birth mother got her life together and asked for custody.

As Ginger rocked the baby to sleep, tears rolled down her cheeks. She asked God to give him good health and parents who loved him and honored the Lord, and finally, with every ounce of her being, she humbly asked the Lord to allow her and David to adopt Joey.

Case workers were skeptical at first, but they allowed the adoption application to proceed. The Clausens' hopes were raised when they learned they could adopt Joey before his first birthday, but red tape slowed things for more than a year. Their patience and steadfastness were rewarded when just after his second birthday their little boy officially became Joseph Albert Clausen.

Since then the Clausens have adopted two girls, Kimarie and Carolyn, who originally came to them as foster children. God has granted the desire of their hearts.

I asked the Lord to give me this child, and he
has given me my request (1 Samuel 1:27).

A PICTURE IN A PORTRAIT

23.

· *wheels up* ·

God's grace for mothers is not limited to whether they are "stay-at-home" moms or "working" moms (since they're all working moms!) But when a true "God thing" occurs, you'll often see it affect the big picture. It confirms an important decision that weighs on your heart and needs God's hand of guidance. The following story about Shelley's struggle illustrates this truth perfectly.

Shelley Shrader struggled with the question millions of working mothers have asked: "Is my career worth it?"

Married at twenty-one, with another year awaiting her at the University of Texas at Arlington, Shelley wanted to enjoy life with her husband, Greg—just the two of them—before kids changed their lives forever.

After college, the couple moved to Fort Worth, where Shelley joined American Airlines as a flight reservationist. Greg began working in the data processing department at DynCorp, a defense contractor. Shelley didn't like being desk-bound, so she applied to become a flight attendant. She received her wings in 1990, four years into her marriage.

Flight attendant work, she discovered, was more difficult than it looked, and less glamorous than it was made out to be. Serving 125 people dinner in one hour was a trick. Work hours and layovers were long, and passengers took out their travel frustrations on their nearest targets—flight attendants. Shelley often felt like a doormat at thirty thousand feet.

One evening, Greg and Shelley discussed their future. "Remember how one of my goals was to have children before I was thirty?" Greg began. "Well, I'm nearly twenty-nine, so if now is a good time . . ."

Shelley, two years younger, nodded her agreement. "I wasn't mature enough to have kids when we married, but I'm ready now."

Lauren arrived in 1994. Eric joined the family three years later. Shelley juggled flight and day-care schedules. She wanted to enroll Lauren in her church's preschool program, which met from nine A.M. to two P.M. on Tuesdays, Wednesdays, and Thursdays, but she couldn't guarantee that those would be her off days. Flight attendants generally crossed the country three to four days a week.

When Lauren turned four in August 1998, Shelley tried to "give up" her scheduled trip to a co-worker wanting a few extra hours, but she had no takers. Then she offered extra money for anyone to take her trip. Still no takers.

Her new work schedule for September and October showed Shelley working three out of every four weekends. The holiday season was just around the corner, and Shelley didn't want to be away from the family on Christmas morning again. What would be best for her family? She began to pray in earnest.

Shelley worried that if she quit work, frustrations would billow and she would be a worse mom. She kept thinking, *Don't I need the stimulation of the business world? Wouldn't I be a better mom if I got a break?*

She sought out the advice of a friend, Linda Eslick. "I'm so confused about what I'm supposed to do," Shelley said. "I just saw the doctor for my tension headaches, which he attributed to stress."

"Tension headaches are not a good sign," said Linda sympathetically. "One thing I've learned is that God has always provided. It might not be the way I hoped things would turn out, but He has provided."

Shelley was heartened. She took Linda's words to mean that if she put all her faith and trust in the Lord, He would not fail her. *Perhaps God is using this situation to increase my faith in him,* she thought.

For two weeks, Shelley agonized over the decision. "Lord, please let me have peace. Please let me be assured that this is the right thing."

She decided to quit and worked her last day on December 1, 1998. Leaving American wasn't all that bad: Shelley's seniority qualified her for an "early retirement" plan that allowed two flights a year for her and her family anywhere the airline flew.

The money? The Shraders would have to tighten their belts, but having Mom home was the best thing to happen for Lauren and Eric.

Early in January, Greg came home from work and enthusiastically invited Shelley out for dinner. At the restaurant he handed her an envelope. "I got this at work today," he said.

The letter, marked "Private, Confidential," noted that Greg's salary had been frozen for two years, but now, based on his excellent work performance, he was receiving an annual increase of $17,000.

"That's what I was making with American!" Shelley exclaimed.

Shelley had followed God's leading to leave American Airlines, and when she and Greg least expected it, the Lord made up the shortfall to help her stay home with her children. Her new career as a full-time mom was cleared for take-off.

Even strong lions sometimes go hungry, but those who trust in the Lord will never lack any good thing (Psalm 34:9).

24.

· *peggie's place* ·

Few things are more important to pray for than a sign of God's will as it relates to a lifetime spouse. The potential joy and the potential heartache are so strong that no one should settle for a second-best, rushed decision. Sadly, many are in too much of a hurry to wait. But when God is asked to take the reins, I've discovered that the loneliness of waiting never compares to the joy of giving Him time to send His very best.

"When God puts a hesitancy in your heart, it's usually because He wants to do something different with your life."

Standing on the doorstep of adulthood, Peggie Coletti thanked her father for his advice, then retreated with a mixed bag of emotions to her bedroom. Her parents didn't have the money to send her to the Christian college of her dreams, and now uncertainty about the future troubled her.

Alone in her bedroom, she opened *Streams in the Desert*, a

book of daily inspirational readings by Lettie Cowman. On the page for that day, February 5, her eyes fell on a poem based on the story of Ruth and Boaz in the Old Testament. (Ruth was a destitute widow who left her own country to care for her mother-in-law in a foreign land. There, God blessed her with marriage to Boaz, a godly, wealthy landowner.)

What she read succinctly demonstrated how God can and does support His people in times of crisis, trial, and tragedy. One short verse from the Book of Ruth made a lifelong impression: "Sit still, my daughter."

Okay, Lord, I'm going to sit still.

Peggie stayed home and worked as a legal secretary while helping her father, a pastor of a small church in Pennsylvania. She led the church youth group, visited the sick, and directed the choir. Romances blossomed several times during her twenties, but quickly withered.

I'm going to sit still, Lord.

By the time she rounded her thirtieth birthday and then hit her mid-thirties, Peggie wondered if she would ever meet the man that the Lord wanted her to marry.

After another romantic relationship soured, Peggie turned to the Book of Ruth for more comforting words. "Lie down until the morning," she read in chapter 3, verse 13. It seemed God was telling her to rest during this period of discouragement. He was promising that joy was coming "in the morning."

On another occasion, after Peggie had received a "this-isn't-working" missive in the mail, a retired missionary wrote her a friendly letter that finished with this statement: "My prayer for you is Ruth 1:9." The verse said, "May the Lord grant that each of you [Ruth and her sister-in-law] will find rest in the home of another husband."

Okay, Lord, I'll lie down until the morning.

A matchmaking friend tried to introduce Peggie to Joe Bohanon, a thirty-seven-year-old professor at a Christian college, but they never went out for one reason or another. Eventually, however, Peggie attended a conference where she saw Dr. Bohanon. They introduced themselves and, after chatting, took seats next to each other.

At the close of the session, the speaker asked those with prayer requests to stand. Peggie had a sinus problem, but most of all, a "special unspoken need."

The speaker then inquired if those nearby could pray for their neighbor. Joe quietly prayed for Peggie, not knowing the personal nature of her "need."

Three days later, Joe called. Over the next few weeks, their friendship flourished under a parade of flowers, presents, and dinners. Within three months, Joe asked Peggie to marry him.

During their engagement, Joe and Peggie attended a breakfast meeting. The master of ceremonies, who knew Joe and had just learned of his engagement, asked Joe and Peggie to stand in the crowded conference room.

"The Lord has a word for you," he began, "and he has showed me that you, Joe, are her Boaz, and Peggie is the one prepared from the foundation of the earth to be your helpmate. A blessing will come out of this union."

At that moment, fifteen years of promises from the Book of Ruth came together in Peggie's mind. Joe, at six feet, seven inches tall, was her "tower of strength." He was sensitive to those in need, and showed a keen sense of responsibility.

Completing the "Ruth and Boaz" theme on their wedding day, Joe and Peggie decorated the church with sheaves of wheat to symbolize how God had brought them together.

Peggie is creator of the very popular www.peggiesplace.com Web site.

Weeping may go on all night, but joy comes
in the morning (Psalm 30:5).

A PICTURE

25.

· *turning a corner* ·

Have you ever wondered if there has to be more to life than what you are currently experiencing? I have. I get caught in that proverbial forest, and I can't seem to find the trees. If you ever wonder whether life has meaning beyond the mundane, and purpose above the inner pain, look for something. Look for God to speak, tell Him you're listening, then get ready to experience your own "God thing."

Duane Brannon had a great job, a wonderful wife, four beautiful children. Why was this middle-aged dentist feeling so restless and dissatisfied? On the outside, he "had it all," but on the inside, he needed . . . something more. To identify what it could be was beyond him.

One Saturday, Duane thought it would be a nice change of pace to invite the entire family out for lunch following church the next day on the Memorial Day weekend. "We can drive down to Old Town and eat at the Casa De Bandini," he said, referring to a classic Mexican restaurant in San Diego's restored Old Town quarter.

"It's too far," one child complained.

"I don't want to go either," chimed in his teenager.

"Let's make this a special occasion," Duane persisted. "We can get all dressed up and have a special meal out."

The next day, the children still registered mild protests as the family Suburban headed south for the thirty-minute drive. On this holiday weekend, however, it seemed as if *everyone* had the same idea—eat authentic Mexican food at one of the restaurants ringing the pioneer square at Old Town. Nearing Casa De Bandini, they found no place to park.

"Why don't you take the kids and put our name in," Duane said to Becky. "I'll try to find a place to park this beast."

For ten minutes, Duane drove up and down the narrow streets. Finally, he gave up and headed several blocks northeast of the restaurant, a good ten-minute walk. Duane parked the Suburban and began walking briskly in what he thought was the direction of the restaurant.

Walking up one block, he realized that he had passed the right street. Should he turn around? *No,* he thought. *I'll just make a right at the next corner and work my way over.* He stepped up his pace, knowing Becky and the kids were waiting for him.

Up ahead someone was making a scene—*another one of those crazy homeless men,* Duane thought. As he approached, however, he saw that the man was dressed in combat fatigues. He pegged him at fifty years old, with his gray beard. *A Vietnam veteran?*

Maybe twenty-five people sat on the sidewalk or stood listening to the veteran as he implored the crowd, "Don't forget the veterans this Memorial Day weekend! This is not the time to forget our comrades who made the ultimate sacrifice on behalf of our country."

Duane noticed a small memorial statue and plaque—and very little space to walk through. He decided to stride quickly in front of the veteran, who was calling out names of San Diego County men killed in Southeast Asia.

Just as Duane passed directly in front, his ear twelve inches from the veteran's mouth, the former soldier loudly proclaimed, "Jack Davis."

Jack Davis?

Duane stopped in his tracks and looked at the veteran. Jack Davis had been Duane's good friend at Fallbrook High School in San Diego. Jack was killed in Vietnam when his helicopter went down. Instantly, Duane recalled Jack's big smile and what a good buddy he had been. Losing him had been devastating.

Then Duane was jerked back from the reverie. What were the odds that Jack's name would be called out at the moment

Duane passed directly in front of this veteran? Had God orchestrated this event on a Sunday afternoon?

Duane knew the answer. God had wanted to remind him of Jack, who died so young without ever experiencing the love and closeness of a wife and children.

What did Duane have to complain about? So what if he was down in the dumps!

God had made an appointment for Duane to learn an invaluable lesson. From that "chance" moment, he understood that life was God's gift to be appreciated every day.

> Jesus said, "Come to me, all you who are weary and
> carry heavy burdens, and I will give you rest. Take my
> yoke upon you. Let me teach you, because I am humble
> and gentle, and you will find rest for your souls"
> (Matthew 11:28–29).

26.

· *listening to God* ·

Have you ever had an emptiness come over you in response to a prayer? When God senses an earnestness to your prayers, He is very serious about answering . . . but not always in the way you expect. If you were to pray for new ways to become intimate with God, you might expect to get more out of the Bible, see rainbows through the thunderstorms of life, or witness God do a miracle through you. What happened to Diane no one could have predicted . . .

Strangely, people were mumbling more. No matter how hard she listened, Diane could pick up only bits and pieces of phone conversations or friendly chatter. A hearing specialist finally confirmed her fears: "Young lady, you are going deaf."

Until then, Diane Comer's life seemed close to perfect. Raised in a loving home, she married a pastor and had three healthy children by the age of twenty-six.

Diane had become a Christian while a teenager, followed the faith, and lived what appeared to be an exemplary life. But still, an emptiness nagged at the edges of her heart.

Laurie Keyes and Alice Wilhelm, fresh from overseas missionary assignments, reached out to Diane in their women's Bible study at church. Their mentoring prompted Diane to begin praying that God would lead her to a deeper intimacy with him. She asked God to do "whatever it takes."

Soon afterward, Diane heard the doctor's diagnosis loud and clear. *Deaf? With three young children? How will I be what my family needs me to be?*

As days and weeks passed, Diane's hearing slowly declined. Doctors could find no cause, no cure. For reasons unknown, the cochlear nerves in both ears were disintegrating.

At first, it was the little things. She couldn't hear the telephone ring if she was in another part of the house. And if she answered the phone, she couldn't be sure with whom she was talking. All voices began to sound the same. Once she carried on a fifteen-minute conversation with Stacey, only to discover she was talking with Lucy.

Diane could hear—she just couldn't understand what she heard. With a group of people at church or a restaurant, she had to work hard to wring out every intelligible bit of sound from the roar that met her ears. She often went home exhausted by the effort, or embarrassed.

Well-meaning individuals told her, "But you do so well—nobody would ever know!" What they didn't know was how much she missed, how often she bluffed, how tense she felt in conversation, how many people she avoided for fear of having to say, "I'm sorry, but I can't hear what you're saying . . ." She felt stupid every time she saw that look in their eyes that meant she had blundered.

But Diane's home was no refuge, either. There she felt the worst pain. When her baby cried at night, she couldn't hear the need. When her toddler wrapped her dimpled arms around Diane's neck and whispered sweet secrets, she couldn't hear the love. When her son told her all about his first stay away from home at church camp, chattering away in the car, she couldn't hear the excitement.

Of course, not hearing birds or crickets or alarm clocks wasn't so bad. But those lovely, intimate, important words . . . she longed to hear. She had to hear!

Diane began to sink into depression. She had never experienced such sadness before. Difficulties before this she had handled almost cheerfully, but this was darkness. She couldn't "just cheer up." Fear, anger, and most of all self-pity overwhelmed her.

Why had God turned his back on her? How could He allow this to happen?

She prayed, and felt only silence. She read her Bible, and wept. She wrapped herself in a cloak of despair, and firmly shut everyone out.

Finally, Diane asked the elders of her church to pray for healing. As these men surrounded her with prayer and anointed her with oil (a practice that the Book of James in the Bible recommends), the darkness that seemed to cloud her vision lifted. Brilliant light broke through the despair. She sensed clearly the voice of God speaking to her heart. And in that instant of illumination, she knew that His answer was no—no miraculous healing of her ears, but an instantaneous healing of her heart. God's peace invaded her life; her heavenly Father was by her side.

Early the next morning Diane woke up and began reading her Bible. This time God spoke to her through Scripture:

> *I waited patiently for the LORD;*
> *he turned to me and heard my cry.*
> *He lifted me out of the slimy pit,*
> *out of the mud and mire;*
> *he set my feet on a rock*
> *and gave me a firm place to stand.*
> *He put a new song in my mouth,*

a hymn of praise to our God.
Many will see and fear
and put their trust in the Lord.
               —Psalm 40:1–3 (NIV)

Diane had heard from God. His "no" left her filled with more peace and joy than she had ever experienced before.

Several years later, Diane retains only 15 percent of her hearing. But as the voices of those she loves grow dimmer, the voice of the One who will never leave her or forsake her grows clearer with each day. The intimacy with God she once craved is hers now—Diane knows she's never alone.

> God has said, "I will never leave you. I will never
> forsake you." That is why we can say with confidence,
> "The Lord is my helper, so I will not be afraid"
> (Hebrews 13:5–6).

A PICTURE

27.

· *cartoon character* ·

*After speaking at large festivals and conferences for more than
thirty years, I can attest—a million times over—that God
sweats the details. In the following story, a man needed a practi-
cal miracle to use his God-given gifts. Guess what? God knew
what he needed, when he needed it.*

"Ralph" was a cartoon character antihero who poked fun at the
school administration and tweaked Establishment noses—perfect for the mid-1970s at the University of Nebraska, where Ron
Wheeler had persuaded the student newspaper to publish his
first comic strip.

Fellow students told Ron there was a lot of truth in his cartoons, but deep down he wondered if they were right. He decided to set off on a course to find out "What Really Matters."
He scaled mountain peaks, jumped out of airplanes, and at-

tended Mind Dynamics seminars. He purchased a hot sports car and found willing women to fill the passenger seat.

None of these pursuits satisfied his hunger for truth.

Ron had wrapped his persona into that of a cartoonist, which was a tough way to make a living. After years of rejection, he discovered that what he was missing was Jesus Christ—not his own syndicated Sunday newspaper comic strip.

Hearing a presentation of the Christian message to make peace with God using the bridge of Jesus Christ, Ron trusted Christ as his Savior and began reading the Bible. When he fathomed that his pride and selfishness had kept him from experiencing God's love, he stopped trying so hard to become a cartoonist. In fact, he was willing to give up the dream altogether.

By "coincidence," the very next day, Ron got his first full-time job, drawing cartoons for a slide show production company right across the street from his apartment.

Ron is now a freelance cartoonist. One of his first clients was the American Tract Society, which in the early 1980s found his humor in comic-book-like tracts effective. Tracts are small booklets handed out to people to explain something about the Christian faith when a long conversation isn't possible. People will read tracts, especially tracts with cartoons in them, when they won't take time to read anything else.

After several years, however, the ministry had a change of leadership, and Ron's tract work abruptly halted. He shrugged and returned to the drawing board. Though his job changed, one thing never changed over the years for Ron: tight finances. When he later began creating CDs containing his cartoons in a clip art format, this entrepreneurial effort stretched him to his financial limits.

Then his balky computer, which Ron uses to manipulate images and even "draw," began showing signs of permanently crashing. Ron's three-year-old Macintosh operated behind the curve: the processing speed was too slow and the hard drive storage unable to meet the demands placed on it.

With a huge poster assignment deadline looming on the horizon, Ron wondered if he should charge a new computer on his Visa card and worry about paying for it later. If he decided to pull the trigger, Ron figured he needed to buy an Apple Macintosh G3 with 266 MHz and a 6 gigabyte hard drive.

Ron began to pray about the situation. Two weeks later, he got a call from Rob Moritz, whose one-man drama ministry as "the apostle Paul" takes him around the country reciting the apostle's New Testament writings.

"Did I tell you I have a new Apple computer?" Rob asked out of the blue.

"Yeah, do you want to give it to me?" Ron joked.

"As a matter of fact I do."

"No, you can't be serious."

"But I am."

"What's it got on it?"

"It's a G3 with 266 MHz and a 6 gig hard drive."

Ron looked down the MacWarehouse mail-order catalog. The same model was staring him in the face.

"No, let me buy it from you."

"I insist on giving it to you. We don't need it anymore, and I know you can put it to good use," Rob said.

Ron drove to Rob's house to pick up the computer. "There it is," Rob said with a sweep of his hand. "You know something? You're going to be amazed when you get to heaven and see how many people were helped in their salvation because of the cartooning gift God has given you."

"I'm overwhelmed, Rob, but I haven't done any gospel tracts in years."

Shortly after setting up the new Mac at his home office, Ron took a call from the American Tract Society. With the new leadership in place, they told Ron they were ready to revise and update their cartoon tract line. Could he revise or create eleven new tracts in two months?

"I sure can," he replied. He had never been asked to do more than four tracts in a year, but with his new computer the assignment was doable.

Then a new client called. Good News Publishers wanted Ron to create five more gospel tracts. God clearly had a plan and His own timetable for getting the message out.

Ron has nearly fifty cartoon gospel tracts in print, and more than 35 million have been handed out all over the world. To learn more about Ron's cartooning, visit his Web site at www.cartoonworks.com.

Whatever is good and perfect comes to us from God
above, who created all heaven's lights. Unlike them, he
never changes or casts shifting shadows. In his
goodness he chose to make us his own children by
giving us his true word (James 1:17–18).

A PICTURE

28.

· the wake-up call ·

Have you ever awakened in the middle of the night and wondered why? If so, you have likely been prompted by God to do something supernatural: pray. If instead you roll over and fall back asleep, does it mean that something bad will happen in the world? I don't know for sure, but I do know that something good can happen if we are sensitive to God's supernatural nudges in the night.

Suddenly awakened at one A.M., Elaine Cunningham couldn't shake the feeling that something terrible was about to happen. Not to Elaine in her comfortable home in the Pacific Northwest, but to her son, John, and his family in Africa.

Pray! The command was urgent. Now wide awake, Elaine sent fervent pleas to heaven. "Please, God, help John and Sandy and the girls. Protect them if they are in danger."

At that very moment, John and Sandy, with five-year-old Sara and three-year-old Jessica, were driving through the *bushveld*, looking for elephants. Sandy was behind the wheel, so that John could take photos.

"It's so hot, Mommy," one of the girls complained. The temperature had already reached triple digits by midmorning.

"I'm sorry, honey, but there's nothing we can do about it," said Sandy. Dust billowed behind the Toyota sedan as the car bumped along the dirt road. John asked the occupants of the few cars they met, "Have you seen any elephants today?"

Finally a positive response: "Go one kilometer and turn left. You'll see some elephants in the river."

Sandy drove down an embankment toward a clearing, veld grass scratching the car's undercarriage. John wondered about snakes. He knew that deadly cobras, black mambas, green mambas, and puff adders inhabited the area. Sandy parked the sedan in a clearing above the muddy river.

"Look, elephants!" Sara spotted them first. John climbed onto the window ledge and looked over the car's roof to get a better view. Even with a telephoto lens, however, he was too far away to snap good pictures.

"I'm going to walk down toward the river," he announced.

"Go ahead, but please be careful. The girls and I will stay in the car," Sandy said.

Stepping onto what looked like a trail, John watched carefully for snakes as he picked his way toward the river. He stopped about a hundred feet from the car and gazed at a small group of cow elephants sucking brown water into their trunks and spraying it over their backs, their huge ears fanning back and forth. Bulls on the riverbank flung red sand high overhead. Calves frolicked in the river, standing with their forefeet on each other's backs. A huge old bull, his tusks nearly touching the ground, stood guard as he moved his head slowly back and forth across the horizon. The view was stunning.

John raised his camera and shot away, wishing that Sandy and his daughters could see this "greatest show on Earth" from his ringside position. That's when he heard an ominous low rumbling like rolling thunder. Looking up and down the river, John saw nothing unusual, but feeling uneasy, he placed the cap on the camera lens and turned toward the car. He stopped dead in his tracks as he realized the source of the noise: a herd of elephants, perhaps more than two hundred! The rumbling was the sound of their running across the dry grasslands.

John's mind raced with pictures of uprooted trees and overturned automobiles. He recalled a missionary's warning never to stand between elephants and their source of water. They become violent if their access is threatened.

Standing between these hot, thirsty animals and their cooling bath and refreshing drink were John and the car holding his family.

Dust swirled in great clouds as the elephants halted momentarily on the crest overlooking the water hole. The herd and John were about equal distances from the car. He faced a quick decision: stay where he was and be trampled, or run for the car and die with his family. Three panic-stricken loved ones screaming from inside his tin can of a car were telling him to run.

Sprinting as fast as he could and ignoring the trail, John raced through the grass and its deadly snakes. He was halfway to the car when the elephants charged.

The first elephants were closing in at full speed as John reached the tiny auto. Jumping in, he slammed the door as the car was engulfed in blinding dust and bellowing elephants. The beasts passed on both sides, rocking the car as they scraped against it. Sara and Jessica screamed in terror as they looked up through the windows and saw nothing but massive pachyderms bearing down on them. John gasped for breath, and Sandy was too frightened to speak. The car jolted back and forth from the thundering vibrations of hundreds of massive feet.

When the last of the herd passed and the dust settled, the car still vibrated from the shaking ground. Every blade of grass and small bush on the hillside was flattened.

Sandy and John tried to calm the girls, then with one voice they thanked God for saving their lives.

"Someone must have been praying for us," John said.

"Only a miracle kept us from being crushed," Sandy agreed. "Let's get out of here!"

Meanwhile, back in America's Pacific Northwest, the hour turned to two A.M. Elaine relaxed as the burden to pray lifted. "Thank you, Father. I know they're in your hands."

Great is the Lord! Your awe-inspiring deeds will
be on every tongue; I will proclaim your greatness
(Psalm 145:3a, 6).

A PICTURE IN A PORTRAIT

29.

· *living in God's economy* ·

Perhaps you've heard the phrase "you can't outgive God." I've found this to be more than true in my own life, especially when what you have to give doesn't appear to be much. When we give cheerfully to God, there is always a reward. Sometimes it's immediate, sometimes it comes back to you in a roundabout way. And sometimes, as this story shows, God makes things happen in an immediate roundabout way!

Australian David Smallbone could make flowers bloom in rocky soil. The Christian concert promoter made a living in a country where Christianity had taken root among only 5 percent of the people.

Then disaster struck. Too few fans filled the seats of a major tour David was promoting throughout Australia. When ticket sales fall short, artists still get their guaranteed money, and the promoter eats the loss. David took a $250,000 bath in red ink.

Creditors swiftly repossessed his house, and the father of six looked for work elsewhere. A top artist asked him to become his manager, with just one catch: he had to move to Nashville, Tennessee, hub of the Christian music industry. Moving without his pregnant wife, Helen, and the children, who ranged in age from one to fourteen, was unthinkable. So, in the fall of 1991, the Smallbones sold their furniture and other possessions and purchased tickets to America.

The fresh start in a new world almost immediately turned sour. The house they had planned to rent was no longer available, so the family bunked together in two motel rooms and survived on fast-food hamburgers until a new rental could be found. Worse, after a couple of months of work, David was informed that his position was "no longer available." He had brought his family halfway across the world for nothing.

David literally could not get out of bed for several days. He and Helen had a "no secrets" policy with the children, and they carefully explained everything that happened. Then they got on their knees as a family and asked God to help them.

All they had was God and one another, plus a roof over their heads. They furnished the house they rented with no more than a few cushions, a table, and a single mattress for Helen, who was now seven months pregnant. Everyone else slept on the floor on beds made out of clothes.

Then the most interesting things happened. Bags of groceries were left at the front door. Acquaintances from the music world took the family out for dinner. Sunday school classes donated furniture. And a Nashville songwriter named Jon Mohr gave the Smallbones—no strings attached—a three-month-old Toyota Previa van with six thousand miles on the odometer.

"It's all yours," Jon said, handing Helen the keys.

Meanwhile, family members took on odd jobs in the neighborhood. Rebecca, the oldest, and two brothers raked leaves and mowed lawns. She also baby-sat and helped her mom clean houses, rarely complaining about disinfecting toilet bowls.

Then came the big break so fitting for Nashville: Forefront Records heard a demo tape of Rebecca singing and offered the fifteen-year-old a recording contract.

Taking on an old family name for the stage, Rebecca recorded her first album as Rebecca St. James, and the family made plans for her concert tour. Jon Mohr knew they needed bigger wheels, so he traded the Previa for a Chevy 15-passenger van. Awestruck by his generosity, David offered Jon 50 percent of Rebecca's "publishing rights"—the money she earned from writing songs.

Flash forward to today. Rebecca St. James has become one of the hottest Christian artists in America. *Christianity Today* magazine has named her one of the top fifty up-and-coming evangelical leaders under the age of forty.

Meanwhile, Jon Mohr and his wife left the music industry to become missionaries in the Ukraine, where they live with their six children. The Smallbones' twice-a-year royalty checks sent directly to the Mohrs' missions account significantly helps support their ministry.

All along—no surprise—God knew what he was doing!

> "For I know the plans I have for you," says the Lord.
> "They are plans for good and not for disaster, to give
> you a future and a hope" (Jeremiah 29:11).

A PICTURE

30.

· *october sky* ·

Like an orchestra conductor who knows the smallest details of a complicated symphony, God has the performance of history—and your life—well in mind. At the right moment, the experienced conductor motions to a section to play louder and a moment later, he signals the cymbals to clash their notes of exclamation. Throughout our lives, God works just like this. Through the high notes and low notes of our particular symphony, God remains firmly in control of the baton.

In the middle of her senior year at Seattle Pacific College, Pat Scofield was called into the business office. She sat down while a school accountant thumbed through her file.

"I'm afraid we can't go on," he announced. "You owe the college too much money. It's not good for us, and it's not good for you."

Pat was dumbfounded. Tight finances had played a role in

her college education all along, but why had money suddenly become an insurmountable barrier to a diploma?

In high school in Oregon, Pat had the grades and the desire to attend Wheaton College, one of the top Christian colleges in the country, but the private school was too expensive for her parents. In fact, her father said family finances precluded much help from them at all.

Pat wanted to become a schoolteacher, so she enrolled in nearby Portland State University. After her freshman year, she transferred to Seattle Pacific College (now University), a private Christian school with a fine academic reputation. Pat's part-time job didn't come close to covering tuition and room and board, but the school's business office allowed her to sign up for a "borrow as you go" loan program.

With graduation now in sight, "borrow as you go" became "you can't go on." Why hadn't something been said before?

"I'm afraid you're going to have to bite the bullet and start paying us back some of what you owe," the school accountant continued.

"But how am I going to do that?" Pat asked.

"Ask your parents for the money."

"But you already know that they are not able to help me financially."

"Perhaps someone in your church can loan you the money."

The conversation was going nowhere.

"What happens if I can't borrow the money?"

"Then you'll have to drop out for a while," he said.

Pat had never felt so dejected in her life. If she dropped out now, she might never return to college and earn her teaching degree. But the more she thought about it, the more she resigned herself to moving back home to Portland and finding a job to pay off her college bills.

A week passed. Pat studied for her finals, sure that her future lay behind some Smith-Corona typewriter in a downtown office pool. Then she was asked to report to the business office again.

"You're probably wondering why you're here," said the man behind the desk.

Pat nodded.

"Have you ever heard of *Sputnik*?"

"Of course," Pat replied. Everyone had. When the Soviet Union launched the world's first satellite, called *Sputnik,* into space on October 4, 1957, the U.S. government and national media reacted hysterically. Something had to be done, or the Soviets would beat us to the moon.

"One of the things that Congress did in response to Sputnik was to pass the National Defense Student Loan Act last summer," the school official said. "Basically, the act calls for more and better elementary school teachers."

"What does that have to do with me?"

"We've decided to make you one of the first recipients of the National Defense Student Loan program. The government will pay for your education, and for each year you teach, the government will forgive ten percent of your debt. Not a bad deal, is it?"

God had used a complicated international situation, the space race, to pave a way for Pat to earn her teaching degree. Following graduation in June 1959, she started teaching the primary grades at Buckman Elementary, a Portland inner-city school.

The story doesn't end there. Pat soon desired to teach at a mission school in Taiwan or the Philippines. Before she could go overseas, however, she was required to take a year of graduate courses at Multnomah Biblical Seminary, where she met a dashing young student from Argentina (*the author of this book!*).

I must have charmed the socks off Pat in our Survey of the Old Testament class, because we married the following summer, in August 1961. After we joined Overseas Crusades, we finished paying Pat's outstanding college education debt. In every detail of Pat's college education, big and small, God was there.

Yours, O Lord, is the greatness, the power, the glory, the
victory, and the majesty. Everything in the heavens and
on earth is yours, O Lord, and this is your kingdom.
We adore you as the one who is over all things
(1 Chronicles 29:11).

A PICTURE IN A PORTRAIT

31.

· *the hiding place* ·

The Holocaust is a tragic mystery I will never understand. I know there are millions alive today who would agree. Was it the natural consequence of a madman given freedom of choice like the rest of us? Could it have been prevented if courageous people—including God's people—had spoken up in the early stages of Nazism? Any answer would be trite and incomplete. The courage of the few who were good did not always outweigh the consequences caused by the many who were evil, but within the darkness there were many lights. This chapter points to a light the world will never forget.

The Weil family was the first to ask the ten Booms to save them from the Gestapo. The ten Booms fixed up several spare rooms— one built with unexpected corners and spaces. A false wall provided a hiding place, allowing the Jews to scramble to safety if the house were suddenly raided. Everyone lived in fear . . .

Corrie ten Boom was born in the Netherlands in 1892, the youngest of four children in a *gzellig* family—Dutch for a pleasant, cozy home in which the family works and plays together. Her father, Caspar, a respected watchmaker in the town of Haarlem, had been raised in a devout Christian home. His father, Willem, was particularly interested in the biblical prophecies that the Jews would one day return to their homeland. Willem passed on his love for the Jewish people to his children and grandchildren.

Corrie, who learned her father's trade, was content to live in her parents' home and work in their first-floor watch shop.

Life changed overnight in the spring of 1940, when the Nazi war machine blitzed through Europe's Low Countries. No one could buy food without ration cards. Dutch newspapers were shut down. Bikes were confiscated and radios turned in, although the ten Booms hid theirs.

All Dutch people fifteen years of age and older were issued identity cards; Jews received a yellow J across theirs. German soldiers smashed the windows of Jewish shopkeepers and pilfered their goods. Jews began disappearing. Rumors swept through villages and towns that the Nazis were carting off Jews to death camps. Aided by sympathizers like the ten Booms, many Jewish families went into hiding.

The day of reckoning came in February 1944.

"Where are the Jews?" screamed the Gestapo major.

"There aren't any Jews here," Corrie answered, lying to save lives.

The Gestapo major belted Corrie, then fifty-two years old, across the mouth. She tasted blood.

"Where is the secret room?"

Corrie didn't answer, except to say, "Lord Jesus, help me."

"If you use that name again, I'll kill you!"

Corrie, her father, and her sister Betsie were arrested, but the Jews who had been hiding in the secret room escaped. Within weeks, her father died in custody, but Corrie and Betsie were dispatched to Ravensbruck, a notorious concentration camp that was home—usually a temporary one because many died there—to 35,000 women.

The roll call siren sounded at four-thirty A.M. In subfreezing temperatures, the shivering inmates often stood in the *Lagerstrasse* until daylight while lines were counted and recounted. Anyone who fell to the ground was pummeled with truncheons and brutalized with kicks. The work was extremely physical: the ten Boom sisters loaded heavy steel sheets onto carts, pushed them the required distance, then unloaded them.

With only a bowl of thin soup, a scrap of dark bread, and maybe a potato to sustain them, the sisters became weaker each day. They knew that if they were committed to the camp hospital, a one-way trip to the gas chambers would soon follow. Everyone could see the tall chimney belching gray smoke from the crematorium.

Corrie had been stripped of every possession except for one item she smuggled into Ravensbruck—a small Dutch Bible. After an exhausting day's work, Corrie and Betsie invited everyone in the barracks to join them for a Bible study.

The guards never intruded. Why? The inmates' beds were crawling with fleas, so the guards kept their distance. Corrie and Betsie thanked God for the fleas.

Corrie managed to keep up with the physical labor demands—nothing short of miraculous given the malnutrition and ill treatment. Whipped by a guard for not working hard enough one day, Betsie was carried off to the infirmary on a stretcher. Two days later, Corrie found Betsie's body dumped in a washroom with other decaying corpses. When she looked into her sister's face, Corrie saw a youthful-looking woman filled with peace and happiness.

Four days after Betsie's death, Corrie's number was called. She was ordered to report to the main office. For what? A trip to the gas chamber? Transport to another camp?

Corrie stood in line. She watched another disheveled woman stand in front of a large desk. The officer stamped a paper and handed it to her.

Entlassen! he barked.

Released? Why was this woman going free?

Each prisoner received the same stamped paper and command. *Could it be true?*

Corrie ten Boom was released from Ravensbruck on the first day of January 1945. It took days to reach occupied Holland by train. Her first real food was tea and a dry crust at a Christian hospital called Deaconess Home.

A young nurse dropped by and asked her where she came from.

"Haarlem," Corrie replied.

"Do you know Corrie ten Boom?"

The nurse, Truus Benes, hadn't recognized the emaciated, hollow-eyed woman as the robust leader of her Girl's Club, which Corrie had organized in Haarlem years ago.

"I am Corrie ten Boom."

Millions of people have read Corrie's biography, *The Hiding Place,* and viewed the movie by the same title, but not many know that Corrie was released from Ravensbruck by mistake, a "clerical error." A few days after Corrie walked through Ravensbruck's iron doors, the order was given to kill all women her age and older.

For the next four decades, Corrie ten Boom crisscrossed the globe, speaking to millions of people about her faith in God that kept her strong under depraved conditions. The nation of Israel also honored Corrie for aiding Jewish people, inviting her to plant a tree in the Avenue of the Righteous Gentiles near Jerusalem.

Those who live in the shelter of the Most High will find rest in the shadow of the Almighty. This I declare of the Lord: He alone is my refuge, my place of safety; he is my God, and I am trusting in him (Psalm 91:1–2).

32.

· *total turnaround* ·

The most amazing "God thing" I've witnessed is God entering the heart of a hurting soul through the healing, forgiving power of His Son, Jesus Christ. I have had the privilege of witnessing this miracle thousands upon thousands of times. When someone makes the choice to open the door of their heart from the inside, unexpected miracles start to occur. Like the one Mike Rogers experienced after one of our events.

Mike Rogers never missed a chance to party at the University of Oklahoma. The only time he felt a pang of guilt was when a fraternity brother, John O'Neal, asked him to join his Bible study. Everyone looked up to John, a defensive back on the Sooner football team, but whenever John asked, Mike averted his eyes and mumbled some excuse about having to study.

Little changed even after graduation, as Mike settled into a career in the insurance business. He dated every woman in sight—and slept with them as well. Although he knew casual sex was dangerous, Mike didn't regard it as sinful behavior. Then again, he wondered why it didn't feel right. He sought advice from his oldest brother, Jim.

"The answers are right here," Jim said, handing Mike a Bible. "Why don't you start reading this a bit?"

Books are usually meant to be read from page one, so Mike started with Genesis. By the time he reached Leviticus, he was totally lost. He put down the Bible, though he occasionally dropped by his brother's church.

Meanwhile, Mike continued to love 'em and leave 'em. On a ski trip in 1997, he met Melissa. They clicked and quickly began spending all of their free time with each other. Melissa was still living with her parents, so Mike usually had dinner at their house, followed by some tennis, a movie, or just watching TV. When Mike and Melissa had the house to themselves, they retreated to her bedroom.

Mike had been down this road many times, and the emptiness in his heart drove him crazy. Then he heard about a coming citywide Christian event. Mike thought that was something he and Melissa needed to check out. Sitting together in the bleachers that night, Mike listened closely while the speaker outlined the steps to becoming a Christian. When an invitation was given to respond to the Christian message, Mike wanted to go forward but couldn't, as if he were paralyzed by the Holy Spirit. He did, however, pray to receive Jesus Christ right there in the bleachers, while Melissa remained standing and singing with her father.

Not much was said during the car ride home, but the next evening, Mike said, "Melissa, I gave my life to Jesus Christ last night, and I'm going to be making some changes, which include not sleeping together."

Melissa nodded, but she remained skeptical. The next Saturday night, when Mike said he didn't want to take her to Erin's Bar to throw darts and shoot pool, she thought he was going overboard.

"Come on, Goody Two-shoes. You gotta have some fun in life."

"No, sweetheart, I don't want to do that anymore."

"Then we could do some other things," she said, drawing close to him.

"No, we're not doing that, either."

Mike never thought he would turn down an invitation to go to bed with a beautiful woman.

Melissa couldn't handle this Christian stuff anymore. While in the car one afternoon, Mike popped a Michael W. Smith CD in the player (he's a Christian recording artist). Midway through the album, Melissa turned down the volume. "We're not going to have to listen to this the whole way, are we?"

"I'd like to, Melissa."

"But I'm tired of this music. I'm tired of the way our relationship is going. All you want to do is study your Bible and go to church. I want to listen to Celine Dion."

Mike and Melissa broke up three times over the next few months. She continued to call him until Mike said, "Melissa, you've got to stop hounding me. It's over, and I'm comfortable with that. You need to make God your number-one priority."

The next day, Melissa called again. "We need to talk," she said.

"Melissa . . ."

"This time it's different. I promise. Can you meet me at the park?"

Melissa was sitting at a picnic table with a Bible when Mike arrived. She didn't turn around as he walked up behind her.

"Mike, I gave my life to the Lord this afternoon," she said, looking up with tears in her eyes.

Mike hugged her and couldn't stop the tears from flowing either. "Tell me what happened."

Melissa recounted a conversation with her dad. When he said she needed to get her life right with God, something in her heart opened up and she asked Jesus to come into her life.

Now, most readers probably expect to read that Mike and Melissa fell into each other's arms, pledged their undying love for each other, and got married. Actually, that has not happened. They don't know what is ahead. But they're confident God is writing the "rest of the story."

What this means is that those who become Christians
become new persons. They are not the same anymore,
for the old life is gone. A new life has begun!
(2 Corinthians 5:17).

A PICTURE

33.

· *the house on the hill* ·

If God gave you something undeserved yet magnificent, what would you do with it? In our society, where many people make more money than 85 percent of the world's population, something undeserved yet magnificent applies to nearly all of us. So . . . what do you do to return God's blessing? The answer, of course, is between you and God. I know what one couple did in Ireland, however, that showed their thanks to God for the miracle He sent.

Robin and Olive Boles met at a youth congress in Belfast in the early 1950s and married in 1959. One of the couple's entertaining pastimes was looking at houses and speculating where they might put down roots and start a family.

Robin first spotted Carrigoona, a large house for sale on two acres of landscaped gardens among the Wicklow mountains, known locally as the "Garden of Ireland," when she took a holiday job.

"Do you think it's too big?" Olive asked.

"Probably, and certainly it's too dear for us," Robin said. "But the house is going on the auction block next month. Why don't we go along, if only to see what price it goes for."

The couple was surprised when Carrigoona did not receive one realistic bid and was withdrawn from auction. Olive knew the vendor's solicitor (attorney) and gave him a call.

"Want to take a look?" he asked.

Why not? Robin and Olive inspected the house and fell in love with it. Like most young couples, they had very few savings, but they felt the Lord was driving them to purchase the property. They put together an offer of $3,685.

"I'll tell you what I'm going to do," said the solicitor. "I'll forward your offer with the recommendation that it be accepted in the absence of any other bids."

Family and friends thought they were crazy to contemplate the purchase of Carrigoona, but the couple was confident that if the Lord did not want them to have it, their small offer would not go through.

Three weeks later the solicitor phoned with the good news that their offer had been accepted.

That same afternoon the directors of a nearby film studio toured the property and informed their agent they wished to purchase the house, making it clear that "money is no problem." When the agent phoned the solicitor to present an offer, however, he was told Carrigoona had just been sold!

Over the next three decades, the Boleses opened their home for the Lord's work. Wanting to help young people who lived in nearby Bray, Olive started a Girls' Club on Thursday evenings. The first week six girls came, and Olive taught them to make an apple tart, gave them a Coke and a sticky bun to eat, told them a Bible story, and encouraged them to bring a friend the next week.

Seven days later, twelve girls were waiting for their ride to Carrigoona. The club quickly grew to thirty-six, the most Olive thought she could handle. She told the girls that if they missed for three weeks, their place would be given to someone else. Very few missed!

Their mothers lobbied for a Boys' Club, too, and thirty-six boys soon were gathering on Wednesday nights.

"When are we going to get our own club going?" one mum asked, and the Ladies' Club began meeting monthly. Later, a monthly Bible study was begun. Olive brought some of her friends to hear a Christian speaker at the Point Theatre in Dublin. At least two of them trusted Jesus Christ as their Savior.

Today there is an active church in Bray called Christians at

No. 5. They meet in a house at 5 Eglinton Road. Many of the original members first heard the good news of Jesus Christ at Carrigoona, the lovely home on the hill that God provided for Robin and Olive Boles.

"You are the light of the world—like a city on a mountain, glowing in the night for all to see. Don't hide your light under a basket! Instead, put it on a stand and let it shine for all. In the same way, let your good deeds shine out for all to see, so that everyone will praise your heavenly Father" (Matthew 5:14–16).

A PORTRAIT

34.

· *not in vain* ·

Five men were killed. Widows, orphans, and extended family members were left to cope. A tragic and senseless event, right? If God had loved these people he would have prevented it from happening, right? Since it did happen, all those touched by it would grow up to be angry and bitter at God, right? All three questions can be answered in the negative. Read on and you will see that because God is the Great Redeemer—even in this life—He is able to make something good out of anything, if people ask and expect it to happen.

In 1997, thirty-four university students from Washington State embarked on a summer trip of a lifetime: an anthropological trek to visit the Huaodani (pronounced wow-DAH-nee) people deep in the Amazon jungles of South America.

When they left for the jungle, the students weren't aware of three very important facts. First, the Huaodani had come to the world's attention more than forty years earlier when several of their tribesmen speared to death five young missionaries. Second, being from state universities and not young men and women of faith, they had never heard the names of the five who were killed: Jim Elliot, Nate Saint, Pete Fleming, Ed McCulley, and Roger Youderian. Third, following that horrific event, many Huaodani came to know Jesus Christ through the efforts of Nate Saint's sister, Rachel.

To reach the Huaodani encampment, the students followed Steve Saint, the son of one of the five martyrs. Steve had spent time living with his aunt Rachel and the Huaodani while growing up and could communicate in their language. Several Huaodani acted as guides to walk the group along the eastern flanks of the Andes mountains in Ecuador and down into the virgin Amazon basin. Their three-day trek along a jungle trail included several downstream stretches in dugout canoes. Steve saw rapport building between the students and their guides.

Finally, the students unloaded their bags at the Huaodani campsite. As they settled around a campfire that evening, a student asked Steve about the "savage Huaodani" they had read about before leaving the United States. Sitting on a log under a star-studded sky, Steve calmly explained, "The very people you have been traveling, eating, and sleeping with—your guides— are, in fact, those 'savages.'"

"That can't be true!" one student exclaimed, as others murmured their agreement.

"But it is," Steve replied. "If you don't believe me, why don't we ask some of these Huaodani where their fathers are."

Taking up the challenge, one student nodded toward a Huaodani woman. Steve translated.

"Boto meampo doobae wendapa," she replied. "Having been speared, he died a long time ago." Her tone of voice suggested that any other cause would have been unusual.

Overhearing the conversation, four more Huaodani volunteered that their fathers had also been speared and killed. One woman, Ompodae, nodded toward an older man a few feet away who was listening to their conversation. His name was Dabo.

"See him?" said Ompodae. "He killed my father and nearly the rest of my family, too."

The students couldn't believe that a woman could talk so calmly about a person—someone sitting a few feet away—who had killed most of her family.

Dawa, another Huaodani woman, spoke up. Pointing to her aging husband, Kimo, she said, "Hating us, Kimo speared my father, my brothers, my mother, and my baby sister, whom my mother was nursing in her hammock. Then he took me and made me his wife."

The visitors were stunned. "How could she live with a man who murdered her family?" one young woman asked.

Realizing that the students did not know about the missionary slayings, he put his arm around Kimo's shoulders and informed them, "Kimo killed my father, too."

This was too much to comprehend. "What changed these people?" a student asked.

Steve knew the answer but wanted the group to hear it from the lips of Dawa, Kimo, and the other Huaodani. They explained how they used to kill inconvenient babies, and how mothers strangled daughters to meet the demands of dying husbands, who wanted their children to keep them company in the hereafter.

The Huaodani explained that evil spirits and witch doctors' curses could kill as effectively as their warriors' spears. They spoke of living in constant fear of being ambushed, even while working in the gardens. Then they explained to these highly educated young people how they learned that the "Man Maker" sent His Son to die for people full of hate, fear, and desire for revenge.

"We now follow God's trail," said Dawa. Then she asked Steve to translate a question for the audience. "All people die, but if you are following God's trail, then dying will lead you to heaven. But only one trail leads there. Have you heard me well? Which one of you wants to follow God's trail?"

There was silence again. A lone hand rose into the night air. Dawa joyously clapped her hands and said, "We will see each other in God's place some day."

Around a campfire in the Amazon, the dawn of the twenty-first century came face to face with the Stone Age—and came up short. In a fleeting but eternal moment, Steve Saint saw the Great Commission of Jesus Christ—"tell people about me everywhere [even] to the ends of the earth" (Acts 1:8)—come full circle. Dawa's witness to the gospel was living proof that his father's blood truly had not been shed in vain.

Go into all the world and preach the Good News
to everyone, everywhere (Mark 16:15).

A PICTURE

35.

· *dutch treat* ·

What would it take for God to get your attention today? Did you know that the God of the Bible is in the "restoration business"? He wants to restore hearts to Himself. I have found He is lovingly persistent in reminding a human soul of His deep affection. Is He in a hurry? Sometimes, perhaps. But I have more often seen Him take His time to get the message across. What is that message? That today is the day of salvation . . . as an elderly couple discovered not long ago.

Clara loved both new things . . . and surprises. Within a week's time, she would get both.

Luke Mulder's idea was to install two skylights in their home outside of Bothell, Washington, while Clara, his wife of thirty years, visited her sister in California. Luke prided himself on his handyman skills. The first skylight went in without a hitch. He moved his aluminum ladder to the living room hallway to tackle the second.

Luke positioned the ladder just so, then decided he should throw a rug underneath it so that he wouldn't scratch the tile floor. *Clara wouldn't like that.* He was standing on the ladder, trying to yank a nail from the ceiling, when it slipped out from underneath him. Luke crumpled in a heap, and his head broke through the drywall.

Dazed and in pain, he considered calling 911, but then they would see how stupid he had been to put a rug under a ladder. They'd probably whisk him off to the hospital, and that would be the end of his skylight surprise.

Luke rolled over, pulled himself up, and hobbled to the kitchen. He filled a bag with ice and shuffled upstairs to bed, where he lay on his stomach and let the ice bag rest on his aching back. *I could have broken my neck . . . I could have killed myself,* he thought. *And if I had died, what would have happened to me?* He pondered that question . . .

Nearly one thousand miles due south, Clara was receiving some well-deserved rest. She had worked herself to exhaustion preparing the food and hosting her youngest son's wedding in their wooded backyard just a week earlier. That made two sons married in her home in seven months, and Clara needed a break. Luke suggested she visit her sister Mieke in California.

All Mieke wanted to talk about was how she had "found Jesus" and become a Christian. "It's been the best thing that ever happened to me," she told Clara, who could tell by the excitement in Mieke's voice that her sister had experienced something special.

Clara was born in 1926 in the Netherlands East Indies, a Dutch colony known today as Indonesia. Her parents called themselves Protestants, but they never entered a church, never had a Bible in the home, and never mentioned the name of Jesus.

In 1942, the East Indies fell to the Imperial Japanese Army, and Westerners were imprisoned in concentration camps. Clara, then sixteen, soon learned what hunger was all about. Daily rations amounted to a slice of dry bread and local greens such as water lily leaves. The women exchanged recipes so they could at least think about meat, mashed potatoes, and raspberry pies.

Two hundred kilometers away at another concentration camp, Luke Mulder was thankful to be alive. A Japanese submarine had torpedoed the Dutch freighter he was aboard. After managing to escape the burning hulk before it sank, Luke survived ten days on the open sea in a crowded lifeboat. They landed on an uninhabited island near Sumatra, Indonesia, but were later captured by the Japanese.

Luke also experienced hunger. One day he caught a handful of frogs, which he and others turned into frog soup. If the Japanese guards had ever found out, he would have been beaten within an inch of his life.

After the war, Clara returned to Holland, where she taught school, and Luke took a job with Dutch Shell on the island of Curaçao in the Caribbean. Feeling adventurous, Clara accepted a position in Curaçao teaching children of Dutch employees. That's when she met Luke, and they married in 1952. After Luke retired in 1970, they returned to Holland, but they found the Dutch people had changed in ways they didn't like. They moved to America because Mieke said it was a nice place to live.

Moaning in agony, Luke knew that if he had died from the fall off the ladder, he would not have gone to heaven. Years ago he had rejected the God of heaven and rebelled against his Christian parents' strict but loving upbringing. Now it was time to come back to Jesus.

"Lord, please forgive me," he prayed as he got on his knees. "I have not followed You, but please have mercy on me. I want to change my life. I want to find a church. I want to study Your Bible."

Though the years had made some things fuzzy, Luke remembered that coming to God in humility and repentance was all that was required to rekindle a dormant faith. After his prayer, he knew he was a Christian.

At the same moment in California, Clara sat in the church classroom with mixed emotions. She had been invited to a women's prayer meeting—an experience all new to her. The women seated around her began to pray one by one for Clara, and as they did, she became drawn to Jesus Christ. That's when Clara realized that her only hope was in God, who loved her unconditionally and was ready to accept her. She opened her heart to Christ and received Him.

On the plane ride home, Clara wondered what she would say to Luke. He wasn't going to understand that from now on she wanted to worship God each Sunday and study the Bible.

On the way to the airport, Luke—sore but okay—carried on a similar conversation in his mind. How could he ever explain what had happened to him?

They fell into each other's arms.

"Honey, I have something to tell you," Luke said.

"No, I have something I must tell you first . . ."

The Lord . . . does not want anyone to perish,
so he is giving more time for
everyone to repent (2 Peter 3:9).

A PICTURE

36.

· *in the rough* ·

Sometimes God chooses the "easy" way to get someone's attention, sometimes the "hard" way. It all depends on how a person learns best. Whether we're a consistent follower or haven't thought about God in years, I'm convinced that God is always there, reminding us to give Him the attention needed to make a difference in our life hour by hour. How do you learn best? There is a golf instructor in Georgia who admits he's had to learn the hard way.

Charlie Sorrell didn't pick up a golf club until he was twenty-one years old. Yet within four years, his splendid hand-eye coordination led him to seek a career as a professional.

After becoming the head pro at Lake Spivey Golf Club in Jonesboro, Georgia, Charlie thought his game was good enough for him to give the Professional Golfers' Association tour a shot. He followed the pro circuit for two years before deciding to stay closer to home with his wife, Joyce, and two daughters.

One Friday morning in 1980, as the head pro at Fairfield Plantation in Carrollton, Georgia, Charlie accompanied several of the club's top amateur players to Moultrie, Georgia, to play in a two-day team competition.

In a motel room that night, Charlie woke and had to use the bathroom. When he tried to roll out of bed, however, his body would not respond. He tried to move his legs. Nothing.

"Guys, I think I'm in trouble," he said in the dark.

His playing partners turned on the lights. "Something wrong, Charlie?"

"Yeah. I can't move."

"Let's take a look."

They tried to roll Charlie onto his side, but the motion caused him to scream in pain. Paramedics were called, and they rushed Charlie to a nearby emergency room, where the attending doctor examined him. "I'm afraid we're going to have to operate on your back right now," he said. "We've got to do something about this."

Something told Charlie, dazed from the horrific pain he was experiencing, that letting a stranger mess around with his spinal cord was not a good idea.

"No, I have to go home."

"I don't recommend it, Mr. Sorrell."

"I don't care what it takes. Get me home."

"Okay, whatever you want."

Charlie was strapped onto a board and lifted into an ambulance for the three-and-a-half-hour journey home. Joyce had called a lumberyard and ordered a four-by-eight sheet of three-quarter-inch plywood for him to lie on.

His doctor came and examined him and talked in ominous tones of "fusing" two spinal disks. Charlie feared the delicate surgery, so he decided to follow a wait-and-see course.

Lying on his back twenty-four hours a day gave Charlie plenty of time to assess his situation. *My goodness,* he thought, *I can't even get up to go to the bathroom. Is my golf career over?*

For the next two weeks, Charlie seriously evaluated his life. He was a forty-one-year-old golf pro with no other job skills. If he couldn't fulfill his duties at the club, he didn't know what he would do.

Charlie prayed. As he did so, he realized that golf, not Jesus Christ, had been number one in his life. He went to church on Sundays, but he didn't have much of a commitment to church, let alone the Lord.

"Lord, if You will let me get up, I promise I will be there for You. Any time I can share this story with people, I will. I confess that I haven't been there for You in the past. But if You will allow me to get up and walk, You will see changes in me."

The next day, Charlie was able to pull himself up and then gradually, with the aid of a walker, take a few faltering steps. Day by day, he walked a little farther—even as far as the Fairfield Plantation pro shop in an attempt to perform his duties. Placing one foot in front of the other, he doggedly pursued the resumption of his career.

After another month of rehabilitation, he felt well enough to start hitting balls again. He was healed! No surgery was ever needed.

Twenty years later, Charlie is running his own twenty-five-acre private teaching facility behind his home in Stockbridge, Georgia. People come from all over the world to spend several days working with Charlie, who was selected National Teacher of the Year by the PGA and named as one of the "Top 100 Teachers in America" by *Golf* magazine.

Doctors who have examined his back can't explain why the two damaged disks healed themselves. But Charlie knows, which is why his story has become part of his daily lesson plan when he teaches golf to friends and strangers alike.

And whatever you do or say, let it be as a representative
of the Lord Jesus, all the while giving thanks through
him to God the Father (Colossians 3:17).

37.

· *one untimely born* ·

> *Is it ever too late to start over? Some people may think so. They may think that if they've lived their whole life separated from God, He somehow doesn't like them anymore. Nothing could be further from the truth. There's a story in the Bible about some workers who were hired at different times of the day. When their pay was given out at the end of work, they all received the same wage—even those hired one hour before quitting time. God has a bigger view of time than you or I. He doesn't grade on a curve, either.*

Clara Ruffin knew only this about her father: George Franklin Lewis was the only child of a schoolteacher and a florist. After schooling, he began an aimless existence marked by recklessness and irresponsibility. What else could explain why Clara and an older brother were born only two months apart to mothers who never married George Franklin?

Clara didn't see her father more than a half dozen times during her childhood. He eventually married Helen, a rival of Clara's mother, who later bore him four more children.

When Clara began attending Tougaloo College in Tougaloo, Mississippi, she joined the college choir. Since they traveled to nice places to perform, she desperately needed a nice pair of shoes. Her mama didn't have the money, so Clara decided to ask the father she barely knew.

"George Frank," she said over the phone, using the familiar form of his first and middle names (Clara refused to call him "Daddy" because he had never been a father to her), "I'm going to be in a concert next Friday, and I need some shoes. Can you wire me some money?"

She listened to his promise to help out. He was earning some money for a change, working a new job at the state hospital, and Clara dared to believe him. She had never asked him for anything before. No matter how poor the family had been, they were not beggars.

But the money never came. The ache of disappointment stayed with her for many years.

A decade passed, and Clara moved to Connecticut with her husband, Richard, and two sons. One day she was visiting her sister, Anne, who lived in Brooklyn.

"Did you know that George Franklin is in the hospital?" Anne said.

"No, I didn't," Clara said. "Let's go visit him," she suggested, curious to know if the years had changed her father.

They found St. Mary's Hospital and were directed to his room. Clara watched her father's eyes narrow in concentration as she approached his bed.

"Hi, George Frank," she said.

"Hi," he returned.

Clara noticed a puzzlement in his eyes. "So, how are you doing?" she asked.

"Fine," he answered. The puzzlement was real. He was straining to remember who his visitor was.

"Do you know who I am?" Clara asked.

"Well," he began, rubbing his chin, "you're some of my people. I can tell by your eyes."

"George Frank, I'm Clara!"

"Clara. Oh, yeah."

Clara wondered if perhaps her new hairstyle, a short Afro, threw him off. But she left the hospital that afternoon knowing her father had forgotten her.

More years passed, and George Franklin landed in the hospital once more. The years of carousing had caught up with him in the form of high blood pressure and diabetes. He lost a leg to amputation, and an infection kept him in the hospital.

Since her last visit with her father, Clara had become a

Christian, and her spiritual awakening prompted her to see him again. This time his eyes were filled with fear and loneliness, and Clara was moved with compassion.

"George Frank, do you know me?" she said, inching closer to his bed.

"Yes," he replied softly.

"Then who am I, George Frank?"

"You're Clara."

"Are you scared, George Frank? Do you feel alone?"

A slight nod gave Clara the answer she expected. His eyes were locked on her.

"Oh, George Frank! You don't have to be scared or alone. If you accept Jesus Christ as your Savior, you won't be alone." Clara paused. "Do you want to accept Him?"

Again he nodded.

"I mean really, because if you do I can lead you in a prayer that sinners like me have prayed. Right here, right now."

"Yes, I want you to do that."

"All right. Then repeat after me."

George Franklin followed Clara in prayer, acknowledging that Jesus was the Son of God, that He died on a cross for our sins, that He rose from the dead, that He would come again to judge and reign in splendor.

"Since God is life, George Frank, you don't have to fear

death," Clara said. "Jesus has said that He will never leave you or forsake you."

Clara wasn't surprised when she learned the next day her father had slipped into a coma. Two nights later, as Clara drifted in and out of sleep, she found herself praying earnestly—as hard as she'd ever prayed in her life—asking God to be with George Frank, until suddenly she sat up in bed.

"It's over," she said to her husband, shaking him awake. The alarm clock read 4:16 A.M. "George Frank is dead."

He had died at 4:14. A new, much better chapter in George Frank's life had just started in glory.

God showed how much he loved us by sending his only Son into the world so that we might have eternal life through him. This is real love. It is not that we loved God, but that he loved us and sent his Son as a sacrifice to take away our sins (1 John 4:9–10).

A PICTURE

38.

· *pennies from heaven* ·

When I hear stories like the next two you are about to read, I picture God up in heaven saying to the angels, "Watch this!" The angels, of course, have seen it all many times. The loving God of the Bible coming through—to the penny—for a follower who stays faithful to Him and His Word.

Their schoolteacher salaries never left Bill and Eleanor Schlegl with a fat bank account or paid for Hawaiian vacations, but they were thankful for always having food on the table for their growing family. As the years passed and college arrived for their son, Bill, Jr., they needed another car.

"I'll make a deal with you," Bill told his son one night. "I'll pay your insurance premiums if you can handle other car expenses."

A couple of weeks later, Bill was sitting at his desk, working the calculator as he wrote checks to pay bills.

"Bill, dinner is ready," Eleanor said, wiping her hands on her apron.

"I'll be right there, honey."

"What's wrong, Bill?" She couldn't help noticing the frown on his face.

"I don't think we can pay all the bills this month. Billy's car insurance put us over the limit—by my calculations, two hundred and fifty-two dollars over the limit."

"What are we going to do?"

"I'm not sure, El. I don't know what to do."

Eleanor glanced at the pile of bills and checks and envelopes scattered across his desk. She noticed a check sitting off by itself.

"What's that?" she asked.

"Our church contribution."

Eleanor patted him on the back. "Bill, you've always paid our offering to God first, and still do. He won't forget us. He's taken care of us all these years, and He's not about to stop now. Something will happen to help us pay these bills."

Bill tried to force a smile. "Let's eat," he said.

The next day in the classroom, as Bill diagrammed a math problem on the chalkboard, the assistant principal walked into the room. This wasn't unusual, because he visited classrooms regularly, but on this occasion he didn't stand in the back and observe. Instead, he walked over to Bill's desk, placed an envelope on his lesson plan, smiled, waved, and walked out.

Bill's curiosity got the best of him. "Okay, class, I want you to do the even-numbered problems on pages twenty-four and twenty-five," he said. Bill sat at his desk and opened the envelope. To his utter disbelief and sheer delight, he found a check from the school district for $252.

The attached note said that after the last teachers' union contract, some faculty had been accidentally omitted from a special raise. The assistant superintendent had discovered the mistake and asked the school board to correct the error.

Some people might label the event pure coincidence, but Bill and Eleanor insist God answered their prayers. More than ever, they know that whatever they give to Him, He always gives back many, many times over.

But as for me and my family, we will serve
the Lord (Joshua 24:15d).

A PICTURE

39.

· *the last-minute enrollment* ·

On the road of life, there are speed bumps. Everything is running smoothly until, seemingly out of nowhere, there's a bump. It's during these bumps in life that "God things" tend to happen. What may look like God's answer to prayer . . . isn't. What may feel like a right decision . . . isn't. But when we hang in there long enough, and trust God to work it out, we find that "God things" happen in ways we never could have predicted.

Everyone told Rick Myatt that God wanted him at Claremont McKenna. *If so*, Rick thought, *God would need to provide.*

In the spring of 1968, Rick was going to *some* school. It was either college or a draft notice—an invitation to Vietnam—in the mailbox.

"What about Claremont McKenna College?" Rick's dad, Cal, suggested. "I did some graduate work there years ago." Claremont McKenna is one of the Claremont colleges located thirty miles east of downtown Los Angeles and one hundred miles south of the Myatts' home in Bakersfield.

"Isn't it expensive?" asked Rick.

"Yes, but it's top notch. You can apply for grant money from the state."

Rick's dad was right—he qualified for a Cal-Grant scholarship, which covered 80 percent of the $5,000 annual fee for tuition and room and board.

A month before the start of classes, Rick attended a Campus Crusade for Christ (a college parachurch ministry) conference and received the names of two other Claremont students who professed faith in Christ. Rick quickly looked them up on campus, but as the school year wore on, the two guys didn't seem all that interested in a ministry to students.

"I feel like I'm the only Christian on campus," Rick told his father during Christmas break.

"Hang in there," Cal replied. "The Lord has you there for a reason."

That spring, several Campus Crusade staff members got in touch with Rick, who arranged appointments for them with friends and classmates. Four students put their faith in Christ.

"Dad, I think we have some positive things happening here," Rick said.

Back home for the summer, he worked as an engineer's aide at

Occidental Petroleum Corporation. Not only did the job pay well, considering he was a college kid, but his office was air conditioned, much to the chagrin of his older brother, Jerry, who worked on a "traffic crew," painting crosswalks in the torrid Bakersfield heat.

During his sophomore year, Rick organized Bible studies in his dorm room and helped stage events where a large number of people could hear the Christian message, including a performance by a Christian illusionist named Andre Kole.

Jerry graduated from UCLA at the end of that school year, and Cal-Grant administrators figured the Myatt family didn't need as much scholarship money. Rick's grant was cut by $1,500— enough to keep Rick from returning to Claremont McKenna.

"We just can't swing it financially," his dad said that summer. "I'm just a high school social studies teacher."

Rick returned to the air-conditioned comfort of Occidental Petroleum and prayed that somehow God would provide the money for his junior year at Claremont McKenna.

Two things happened that caused him to wonder if the Lord was opening other doors: Occidental Petroleum offered Rick a permanent position, and California State University opened its campus in Bakersfield. Rick could work full time with Occidental and take night classes at Cal State.

This looked like God's answer to prayer. Besides, the more Rick thought about it, Claremont was a rich kids' school. His classmates were from the tony environs of South Pasadena, San Marino, and Atherton. Hadn't the scholarship rug been pulled out from underneath him? Maybe it was time to move on.

Or was it?

His heart was still in Claremont, where he was having an impact for God's Kingdom in classmates' lives. So why was God closing the door?

Several Claremont friends called. "I'm not coming back," Rick said.

"Not coming back? Rick, God wants you at Claremont. You *can't* leave."

"Sorry, but I can't go. I don't have the money."

Decision day was September 7, a week before the start of classes. On that day, Claremont McKenna needed to know whether he was returning; if not, they would give his place to a student on the waiting list. Occidental Petroleum was pressing for an answer as well.

Rick decided that if nothing fell out of the sky by September 6, he would accept the Occidental Petroleum position and enroll at Cal State Bakersfield. He pinned his hopes on an unexpected check in the mail. No letter came.

Well, that's it. I guess I'm staying home and working. It doesn't feel right, but that's God's answer.

At eight-thirty that evening, the phone rang for Rick. "This is

Richard Montgomery from the admissions office at Claremont McKenna."

"Good evening, Mr. Montgomery. What can I do for you?" Rick wondered why he was working so late.

"I understand that you're thinking about leaving Claremont."

"That's correct."

"Is money part of the reason?"

"Yes, it is."

"Well, if that is the reason, I've found a scholarship for you. Will that enable you to stay in school with us?"

"It depends on the amount of the scholarship," said Rick, his hopes rising.

"Let's see. Yes, it's for $1,500."

"I'll be there!"

His final two years at Claremont McKenna left no doubt God had good reasons for providing the scholarship money. The continuation of Rick's on-campus ministry not only led students to Jesus Christ but also changed career plans. After graduating with a math degree, Rick entered seminary. He's now the pastor of a thriving church in San Diego.

> But I am trusting you, O Lord, saying, "You are my
> God!" My future is in your hands (Psalm 31:14–15a).

A PICTURE IN A PORTRAIT

40.

· *the unexpected trade* ·

In Acts 7, a disciple named Stephen was brutally martyred while others watched. Was it something about Stephen's death, however, that helped make a Jewish zealot named Saul into the beloved apostle known as Paul?

I wish following God and obeying His will sometimes had different earthly consequences. For Stephen, it meant death. But for Saul, Stephen's death may have played a critical role in leading him closer to a new life in Christ. What man meant for harm, God turned for good. The story on the next few pages shows how God allows a faithful follower to impact thousands in the midst of trial and adversity.

National Football League running back Sherman Smith, the "Sherman Tank," stood six feet four inches tall and packed two hundred twenty-five pounds of the most solid muscle you'd ever want to tackle. His reputation for bowling over defensive linemen raised his celebrity to near-cult status in the Pacific Northwest, where he played for the Seattle Seahawks. Sherman couldn't cross a Seattle street without being stopped, patted on the back, or asked for an autograph. He was treated like royalty.

Without warning, the Seahawks traded their most popular player to the San Diego Chargers. Everything changed for this running back whose Christian faith was as rock solid as his rib cage. Sherman arrived in a city where nobody knew him and nobody cared. He wasn't with the Chargers for more than a few weeks when he blew out his knee. While in rehabilitation, he wondered, *Lord, why did you ship me to San Diego?*

While his knee mended, Sherman participated in team meetings and joined the club on road trips. He also spoke boldly about his faith—fellow Chargers knew exactly where he stood.

Once while flying back to San Diego after a game, Sherman stood in the aisle with a Bible the size of the Ten Commandments tablets in one hand while leading a Bible study for several players. A defensive back named Miles McPherson asked Sherman to move so he could use the rest room.

Sherman didn't know that Miles had a line of cocaine in his pocket and was planning to get high, but he knew his teammate did not have a personal relationship with God. A good-looking party guy, Miles was a single who knew how to mingle.

"Can I get by?" Miles asked.

"What's up, little brother?" Sherman responded.

"Who are you calling little?"

"You!"

"Okay, okay," Miles laughed. They both knew who the big guy was on the plane.

Before he let Miles pass, Sherman asked him point-blank, "If you were to die today, what would happen to you?"

"I would go to heaven."

"How do you know?"

"Look, man, I went to Catholic school for eight years. I wore a green suit every day. I'm going to heaven for that."

"Nah, you ain't going to heaven for that."

"Look, man, we used to have nuns in our school who were five-foot-two, two hundred and sixty pounds, and they used to smack us in the head. I'm going to heaven for that."

"Nah, you ain't going to heaven for that."

"Why not?" Miles asked.

"Let me tell you a story, little brother."

Sherman proceeded to tell Miles about Nicodemus from the third chapter of the Gospel of John. Nicodemus was well educated in Jewish culture and the Old Testament. He had watched Jesus Christ heal lepers, raise a little girl from the dead, and restore the sight of a blind man.

Nicodemus said to Jesus, "Rabbi, we know you are a teacher who has come from God. For no one could perform the miraculous signs you are doing if God were not with him."

And Jesus said to him, "I tell you the truth, no one can see the kingdom of God unless he is born again."

"How can a man be born when he is old?" Nicodemus asked. "Surely he cannot enter a second time into his mother's womb to be born!"

Miles thought about Sherman's message for a long time. On April 12, 1984, after doing cocaine all night, Miles got on his knees and surrendered his life to Christ. He prayed, "Jesus, I ask you to be my Savior today, and I will surrender my whole life to you. I don't want to live for myself anymore. I will do whatever you want me to do. I will be whatever you want me to be."

When Christ became his Savior, Miles stopped doing cocaine, stopped smoking marijuana, stopped cursing, and stopped picking up girls. He also told Sherman what happened. Sherman and two other players began meeting with Miles to study the Bible, helping him learn from the Word of God. When Miles said he wanted to share his faith with others, they said, "Go for it."

Today, Miles McPherson is an outstanding youth communicator who preaches to tens of thousands each year at Miles Ahead crusades.

Miles and Sherman both know now why the "Sherman Tank" was traded from Seattle to San Diego. God had a plan.

Seek the Lord while you can find him. Call on him now while he is near. Let the people turn from their wicked deeds. Let them banish from their minds the very thought of doing wrong! Let them turn to the Lord that he may have mercy on them. Yes, turn to our God, for he will abundantly pardon (Isaiah 55:6–7).

A PICTURE

41.

· *hitchhiking to a safe place* ·

"With God, all things are possible." Is that a trite phrase or the truth? A witness can only testify to what he has seen. As one witness for God, I can say—without reservation—that there are few six-word phrases with more truth in them. I have heard the stories of thousands of people at the end of their rope who reached out for God. And when they did, they quickly discovered that God was already reaching out for them. God's grace works in many ways, but never more powerfully than when someone finally reaches out to firmly grasp the hand of the Savior.

"Why don't you just kill yourself?" Kristi Dougherty muttered as she stumbled out of yet another bar.

Her teenage daughter had walked out on her and went to live with her father. Another man Kristi was living with abused her and told her she was worthless. *Maybe you are worthless,* she thought. *In fact, you have no reason to be alive.*

Kristi had begun drinking heavily in high school. She bragged that she drank a case of beer a day. Then she met a guy, had a child, and tried to deal with life as best she could. Her best coping mechanism was getting drunk or high enough to fall asleep quickly.

In the summer of 1998, Kristi drifted from Seattle to Pasco, Washington, with a few bucks in her pocket . . . and a death wish. Along the way, she visited her mother and then her brother, a crack addict who frequently lived on the streets.

"You can always find clothes and something to eat in the city," he said. "Just ask for the worst part of town and look for a mission."

Kristi didn't want to be homeless; there was no future in that. She needed money to pay for a hotel room, so she took to the streets and prostituted herself—*a first for me,* she grimaced. Then she checked into a threadbare motel with a six-pack of beer and three dollars to her name. Her plan, she decided, was to drink the beer and then slash her wrists with a broken bottle.

When she walked into the bathroom and broke off the top of a brown bottle, she decided it was too early in the evening. *I need to write those suicide notes first,* she thought.

She set down the piece of glass and walked outside, where she spied a tavern down the street. Inside, the bartender gave her three sheets of paper, a pencil, and an ice-cold draft. She made small talk with the bouncer, and before she knew it, she had invited him to her room to drink a few more beers.

Early in the morning, Kristi was awakened by a hard knock on the door.

"Who is it?"

"Hotel manager. You're going to have to go."

"Wait, I got money. I promise."

"If you can't pay me now, you gotta go."

Kristi didn't have the money so she shuffled out the door with a broken beer bottle in her hand. Up ahead, she saw the Blue Bridge spanning the Columbia River between Pasco and Kennewick. She found a place under the bridge, sat down, rolled up her left sleeve, and jabbed the jagged glass at her wrist, causing it to bleed, but not profusely. Apparently she had missed the main artery, so she tried the other arm. Same result.

You can't even kill yourself, she thought.

Wearing black dungarees and a blood-stained white shirt, Kristi stumbled onto the bridge. She looked over the edge and contemplated leaping into the Columbia. *No, I'd probably survive the fall.* She could see the newspaper headline: SUICIDE ATTEMPT FAILS. She kept walking.

Ahead a green eighteen-wheel truck was parked on the shoulder. The driver, an old man, was sleeping.

"Mister, I need a ride to California," she said.

The trucker rubbed his eyes as he pulled himself out of the sleeper behind the seat.

"I can lose my job if someone catches you riding with me," he said.

Kristi shrugged her shoulders.

"Okay, get in," he said. "I have to sleep some more, but you can lie down here." He pointed to the bench seat in the cab and then handed her a blanket.

Several hours later, he fired up the rig and drove west toward Portland. Just outside the city, he pulled off at a truck stop.

"I'm afraid this is the end of the line. You're going to have to catch a ride with someone else," he said. "If you hitch a ride with another trucker, you're going to have to sleep with him, so be forewarned."

He pulled out his wallet and handed Kristi three dollars. "Here. You may be needing this."

Kristi decided to take her chances hitchhiking on the freeway. A man about her age, in his thirties, pulled over.

"Where you headed?"

"I don't know," replied Kristi. "Portland? I want to go to the worst part of town. That's where the missions are."

Kristi soon found herself at the Harbor Light Salvation Army, a women's facility, working in the kitchen. Two days later, someone handed her a gospel tract.

Kristi stuffed it in her pocket, and when her shift was over, she returned to Room 210 and read the tract. In tears and on her knees she prayed, "If there is a God, I ask You to come into my heart. Please do that right now. I need You. If You can forgive me for what I've done and take away all my guilt and shame, I will walk with You the rest of my life."

Kristi repeated that prayer three more times and felt that God had heard her. But what to do next? The following day, Pastor Jeff at the mission invited her to a Bible study and promised to get help for her at a domestic violence shelter.

What put her on the road that turned her life around, Kristi decided, was God sending two unlikely yet kind male drivers who took her to the very place she needed to go, so that she could get her life—and eternity—together. An elderly truck driver who never picked up hitchhikers, and a gentleman who didn't try to take advantage of her. Why did they give her a ride? Kristi only knows that if they hadn't, she never would have reached her appointment with God.

But then God our Savior showed us his kindness and
love. He saved us, not because of the good things we
did, but because of his mercy. He washed away our sins
and gave us a new life (Titus 3:4–5).

A PORTRAIT

42.

· *a better sense* ·

Those reading these pages who appreciate the fact that God places a "call" on specific individuals may also know that He won't place that call without giving an extra measure of grace and skill to accomplish the task at hand. The story that follows shows how creative God is in portioning out His boundless grace to those who have devoted their lives to Him.

When Lillian Doerksen boarded the ship in September 1950, she had no doubts God was leading her to India.

"Dear Lord, if I am to serve you here in India as I believe you want me to," she prayed, "I need you."

A friend at school had told her about the Pandita Ramabai Mukti Mission in Maharashtra, where eight hundred orphans were in need of care. The mission was founded by Pandita Ramabai in 1868. She had been a Hindu before she found the Lord Jesus Christ and devoted her life's work to caring for thousands of starving, destitute girls, many of them abandoned by their families.

When Lillian disembarked the ship in Bombay, a mass of humanity and poverty assaulted her senses. Walking through the dusty streets, she saw desperate mothers lying on the sidewalk with their children, hands outstretched for alms; rail-thin men straining to pull carts through the crowded thoroughfares; and bony cows, aimlessly walking through the fetid streets. Hindu strictures against the killing of cows allowed them to roam at will.

And the smells! The spicy smells of cumin and coriander in the marketplace made Lillian's stomach turn. Then smoky-scented waves of curry-spiced food simmering on street carts blew across her face, causing her to nearly double over.

Fighting nausea, Lillian bowed her head in prayer. "Lord, please sanctify my smeller. I need you to take away my sense of smell, or otherwise I will have to go back on the same ship to Canada."

Lillian opened her eyes and breathed deeply through her nostrils. The smells were gone! She inhaled again. She couldn't smell! As she continued to walk through the packed marketplace, Lillian bent over a bag of curry spice. Again, nothing.

Lillian devoted herself to the orphaned girls of the Mukti mission until her retirement thirty-seven years later. Although her taste buds can savor the food she eats, she still has no sense of smell. None of her doctors has ever been able to explain why. Other than a miracle.

As for God, his way is perfect. All the Lord's promises come true. He is a shield for all who look to him for protection (Psalm 18:30).

A PORTRAIT

43.

· *a child shall lead them* ·

Do all things truly work together for good? As you have seen throughout this book, the answer is "If you wait long enough, they usually do." And although it is difficult to wait, without waiting comes anger, resentment, bitterness, and faithlessness. Is it possible to notice things working together for good without faith? Unlikely. So . . . God simply asks us to be patient and depend on Him to keep His promises.

Three-year-old Brandon was a fussy eater, but this was ridiculous. He loved eggs, pancakes, and sausage for breakfast, but for lunch and dinner as well? If his mother, Karen LeMaster, didn't cook breakfast three times a day, Brandon threw head-banging fits and tried to dismantle every toy in the house.

The LeMaster home had to be "Brandon-proofed," so Karen's husband, Steve, put locks on everything and even installed motion detectors to catch Brandon during his middle-of-the-night mischief prowls.

The parents sought medical help. Tests revealed that Brandon was autistic. Autism, the LeMasters learned, is a developmental disability, the result of a neurological disorder.

Because Karen worked full time outside the home, Brandon's autism presented a problem when she searched for adequate day care for her son. The last day-care director informed Karen that they no longer could handle Brandon and his penchant for pulling the fire alarm.

Karen looked at eight day-care centers in one day, three of them church-based. Although she and Steve didn't attend church, they were open to sending Brandon to a church-based day-care center because of the "good values" and loving discipline he was likely to receive.

During her interview at St. Matthew's Lutheran Church, Karen was brutally honest about Brandon's behavioral problems. "He is hyper, he needs to be watched constantly, and he's autistic," Karen told Rhonda, the day care director.

"Let's give Brandon a try," Rhonda replied.

Although Brandon was still a handful, his parents were amazed at the subtle changes they noticed. On the drive home, Brandon sang choruses he had learned that day. At dinnertime, while his parents and twelve-year-old brother, Christopher, were poised with forks ready, Brandon said, "Wait, Mom. We have to say grace." Then he would bow his head and pray, "God is good, God is great. Thank you for the food on our plate. Amen."

Brandon also insisted on praying before bedtime, putting his hands together while reciting, "Now I lay me down to sleep; I pray the Lord my soul to keep. Guide me safely through the day; wake me in your care I pray."

Karen and Steve were touched by their son's sensitive heart, as was Christopher. One time after picking up Brandon, Christopher said, "You know, Mom, I'd like to go to church."

The LeMasters had never gone to church together as a family. It wasn't that they didn't believe in God; there was just never enough time. But with Christopher's desire and Brandon's budding spirituality, the LeMasters began attending the church where Brandon went to daycare. After a few months, they found Sunshine Community Church, a growing congregation.

Steve's mom was ecstatic that the family had hooked up with a church. When she heard about the Luis Palau crusade coming to El Paso in May 1997, she encouraged Steve and Karen to attend one night.

They didn't seem interested and made no plans to attend, but on the spur of the moment they decided to come to the Wednesday night rally at the Convention Center, along with their boys.

The LeMasters were going to sit near the front, but Brandon's ears were too sensitive to the loud music. Instead, they found seats at the rear of the auditorium, which was packed with more than six thousand people.

When they sat down, Brandon tugged at his mother and pointed to Grandma LeMaster sitting in the row in front of them!

"Grandma, what are you doing here?" Brandon asked.

When Steve's mother turned, the surprise on her face became a huge smile.

Later that evening, the LeMasters stood as a family and walked forward to publicly state their commitment to Jesus Christ. Grandma LeMaster didn't know if she could keep her heart from bursting, she was so happy.

Brandon's behavior has improved considerably since then, but that isn't the biggest miracle, of course. God used Brandon's autism to steer Steve and Karen to church and an interest in spiritual matters. Without Brandon, the LeMasters might have never found a true relationship with God.

But Jesus said, "Let the children come to me.
Don't stop them! For the Kingdom of Heaven belongs
to such as these" (Matthew 19:14).

A PORTRAIT

44.

· to latvia with love ·

Have you ever wondered if you're worthy of God's rich love? Many people do. A life of either ignorance of God's character or intentionally ignoring what you know to be true can make you believe you are somehow unworthy to receive the great love of God. Did you know that God never thinks anyone is unworthy? I can't say that strongly enough! If this book or the story that follows doesn't illustrate this truth well enough, would you do me a favor? Please call, write, or e-mail my ministry (see page 227) and give us a chance—without any pressure—to convince you that God loves you today, tomorrow, and forever. I pray you will.

Like her childhood friends, Kristine Strele, seven years old, was a Child of October. She proudly wore a star bearing the image of Vladimir Lenin, leader of the revolution. She didn't know what it meant. "I just thought Lenin was a great man who loved children," she said.* "That's what we were taught."

When she was a little older, Kristine joined Pioneers—not that she had a choice. Her friends also were members of the Communist student organization. "There was a certain pride to wear the red scarf around my neck," she said, even if everyone else did, too.

But by the time Kristine was sixteen and a student in art school, the sameness of the Soviet system in Latvia left her feeling caged in and insignificant. She discovered not everyone in the world lived such austere, rigid lives. She was a teenager with opinions she couldn't express, a unique person whose identity couldn't stand out. Kristine wanted to be special, to be important, to have friends who admired her.

"We were all potential artists, so no one was any more special than anyone else," she said. "I was looking for friends who would understand me outside of school and the artists' society. And I met people who weren't good friends for me . . ."

Even in Communist-controlled Latvia, a teenager can get in trouble running with the wrong crowd. Kristine's compulsion to

*To receive a VHS copy of Kristine's full testimony, please write to the address on page 227.

be special hit another feeling head on: guilt. The voice of conscience was telling her she wasn't doing "good" things; she wasn't with the "right" people.

Kristine's grandparents were Christians, and although they didn't talk much about their faith, occasionally they took their little granddaughter to church with them. As a result, Kristine grew up believing in God.

"I knew there was somebody more powerful we can pray to when we have a need, and that's all," she said. "When I needed help, I prayed to God, but I didn't know who He was. But the feeling was growing quite strong that I should do something more worthy of believing in God."

That's when Kristine decided it would be a good thing to sing in a "spiritual choir," and she ended up in her grandparents' church, Saint Matthew's Baptist Church, Sunday morning, September 10, 1989. Gorbachev's *glasnost* had opened doors for Christian speakers in five cities of the Soviet Union, including Riga, the capital of Latvia.

"When I asked my mom which choir I should go to, she suggested Saint Matthew's," Kristine said. "Interesting thing, when my mom was a teenager, she was singing in the choir because of her parents. Later, when she got married, she walked away from God. But the choir was still in her memory as something special."

Kristine had been in the choir only a couple of weeks when it was announced a special service was coming. "We will have this evangelist—everyone please wear white blouses or white shirts."

"I'm glad it happened soon, because I was desperate," Kristine said. "There wasn't peace in my heart. As he was preaching, it seemed as if he knew exactly what was happening in my life. I understood one thing: I needed forgiveness. My life hadn't been right, not the way it should be, and I finally heard that I could say no to my past and start a new life with God.

"As he invited people to come forward who wanted to have Jesus in their life, my heart was starting to beat really fast. I thought, if I stay in my seat I'm going to explode. My knowledge of things was very small, but it was so powerful that one thing I understood: I need Christ."

Fluent in English, Kristine began serving as a translator for Western missionaries who came to Latvia when the Iron Curtain lifted. One young man about to graduate from Bible college in Canada needed someone to translate the Bible studies he was teaching out in Latvia's countryside. Dustin Peterson asked for Kristine.

Kristine had a hunch this was more than a ministry opportunity. She prayed a long time before she accepted the job. Dustin and Kristine eventually married and are teaching the Bible and translating Bible study literature in Latvia as missionaries with Greater Europe Mission.

"I feel very special," Kristine said. "I'm special because I have the Lord, because I can talk with him and He lives within me. And I feel very special that I can serve God."

So now we can rejoice in our wonderful new relationship
with God—all because of what our Lord Jesus
Christ has done for us in making us friends
of God (Romans 5:11).

A PICTURE AND A PORTRAIT

45.

· *over the years* ·

And finally, two stories from my own life; two of many I could tell of how God is intimately aware of the pictures of my life, yet just as aware of the portrait He is creating.

After my father died when I was only ten years old, my family plunged into poverty, and eventually I became the breadwinner, responsible for my mom and five younger sisters. I was still a teenager when the Bank of London in Buenos Aires gave me a trainee's position. Everything I earned went to the family to pay bills—it seemed we owed money to everyone.

On a day when I didn't even have money for the bus ride downtown, I prayed, "Lord, I'm going to trust You to get me to work. I want to test whether You will answer my prayer." I figured the Lord would answer by providing the money—somewhere from my home to the bus stop I would find ten pesos.

On that dark, foggy morning, I walked slowly all the way to

the bus stop, searching the pavement for money. When I didn't find any, I decided to walk a little farther into town to the next bus stop. Not a peso.

I was getting discouraged and thought, *I don't have enough faith, that's all. I'll keep walking.*

Just then I saw a fellow trying to get an old car out of a garage to start it. "Would you like a hand?" I called out.

"Yes, please," he said.

I helped him push the car out of the garage and down the hill. The car started and disappeared into the fog. I kept walking, still looking for my ten pesos.

A few minutes later I heard an idling car. "I'm really embarrassed," the driver said. "You helped me push my car and then I left you. Where are you going?"

"Right into the heart of town. I work at the Bank of London."

"I work at the bank across the street," he said. "Come on, hop in."

There was my answer to prayer! Today that seems an awfully simple answer, but it was the first time that God clearly answered my prayer. Different from what I expected, but He answered.

A much more dramatic story took place a few years ago. I had accepted an invitation to conduct a speaking tour in Peru, South

America, during what ended up becoming a very precarious time in that nation's history. Maoist *Sendero Luminoso* (Shining Path) guerrillas pushed the country to the brink of anarchy, wiping out entire villages, executing military and civil authorities, and martyring religious leaders by the score.

In Shining Path's bloody attempt to overturn the Peruvian government and create a "new society," the terrorists turned their attention to the capital city of Lima, a teeming metropolis of seven million people. The guerrillas targeted American symbols to gain Washington's attention, invading United Press International offices, blowing up an American-owned department store, and even attacking the American Embassy.

I found myself in a panic-stricken country with speaking engagements booked solid for two weeks.

My meetings in Peru's second-largest city, Arequipa, concluded without incident. As I walked out of the last meeting, several envelopes were pressed into my hands. I put them in my pocket for later reading. Later in my hotel room I remembered the envelopes and pulled them out, expecting to read letters of thanks from individuals whose lives had been changed in some way. A colleague noticed when I suddenly tensed up. "What's the matter?" he asked. One of the notes I had just opened was a death threat from the Shining Path. I was warned to leave the country within twenty-four hours or "die like a dog." I didn't know exactly what it meant to "die like a dog," but I wasn't eager to find out.

After much discussion, my colleagues and I decided to proceed anyway. Security was tightened, but there's only so much you can do to guard against terrorists.

The first night at Lima's Alianza Stadium, thirty thousand packed the stands to hear how God still changes lives today. The crowd gasped when they heard a series of explosions in the distance. The stadium lights flickered, yet—thank God—remained on. The rest of Lima, however, was suddenly plunged into darkness. Shining Path guerrillas had blown up electrical power stations throughout the city in an attempt to shut off our power supply, but the only place the lights remained on was the neighborhood surrounding Alianza Stadium!

Grateful that we didn't have thirty thousand people panicking to reach for the exits, I breathed deeply and continued speaking with an extra sense of urgency, thankful that God had miraculously kept the lights on. I told those assembled that this was a time when a decision for God could *not* wait.

[R]emember the former things of old; for I am God, and
there is no other; I am God, and there is none like me,

declaring the end from the beginning and from ancient times things not yet done, saying, "My counsel shall stand, and I will accomplish all my purpose," calling a bird of prey from the east, the man of my counsel from a far country, I have spoken, and I will bring it to pass; I have purposed, and I will do it (Isaiah 46:9–11 RSV).

· *acknowledgments* ·

All praise to God, for whom "everything is possible" (Matthew 19:26).

Thanks to my editor, Trace Murphy, and to my agents, Greg Johnson and David Sanford, who believed in this book and encouraged me to tell these stories.

Thanks to Mike Yorkey for talking at length with scores of individuals and working so hard on many of the chapters in this book. Thanks also to Greg Johnson, Mike Umlandt, Holly Hudson, and Christine Skultety for their invaluable editorial assistance. Additional thanks to Steve Halliday, Debbie Hedstrom, Diane McDougall, and Stephen and Amanda Sorenson.

Thanks to the thousands of people around the world who have shared their stories with me in recent years.

Special thanks to my son Keith and my wife, Patricia, for helping me select the stories to feature in this book.

· *we'd love to hear from you!* ·

Do you have an amazing story to tell? Did God work a miracle in your life or the life of a close friend or family member? If so, we'd love to hear about it! Tell us your story in your own words and send it to:

Luis Palau
P.O. Box 1173
Portland, OR 97207
Fax (503) 614–1599
E-mail palau@palau.org
Web www.lpea.org

· *more true stories!* ·

To receive more true "God thing" stories via e-mail, please sign up for our new electronic newsletter. Once or twice a month, you'll receive a new inspirational "Look at what God did!" story via e-mail.

To request your free e-zine subscription, simply send an e-mail note to Godthing-subscribe@lists.gospelcom.net with only the words "subscribe Godthing" in the body of the e-mail. Or use the handy subscription form at http://www.lpea.org/sub-scription.shtml.

And while you're online, be sure to look for more stories at http://www.lpea.org/Godthing.shtml.